AFRICAN WRITERS SERIES
Editorial Adviser · Chinua Achebe

9

Modern African Prose

AFRICAN WRITERS SERIES

MODERN AFRICAN PROSE

An anthology compiled and edited

by

RICHARD RIVE

Illustrated by Albert Adams

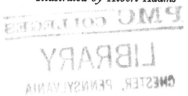

HEINEMANN

LONDON IBADAN NAIROBI

Heinemann Educational Books Ltd
48 Charles Street, London W1X 8AH
PMB 5205 Ibadan · POB 25080 Nairobi
MELBOURNE   TORONTO   AUCKLAND
SINGAPORE   HONG KONG

SBN 435 90009 9

Notes and Introduction © Richard Rive 1964
First published 1964
Reprinted 1965, 1967, 1969

Printed by St Paul's Press Ltd, Malta

For Anthony of Welton and the
thousands of other students on the
Continent like him

CONTENTS

ACKNOWLEDGEMENTS

For permission to reproduce copyright material thanks are due to Faber & Faber Ltd for *The Location* from *Down Second Avenue* and *The Complete Gentleman* from *The Palm Wine Drinkard*; to William Heinemann Ltd for *Father and Son* from *No Longer at Ease*, *The Little Missionary* from *The Tame Ox*, and *School at Sagresa* from *The African*; to Crown Publishers Inc. for *The Park* and *Echoes*, both from *Quartet: New Voices from South Africa*; to Seven Seas Publishers for *Resurrection*; to Victor Gollancz Ltd for *Journey to Blantyre* from *Road to Ghana*; to 'The New African' for *Her Warrior, Eleven o'clock: the Wagons, the Shore*, and *The Martyr*; to Hutchinson & Co. (Publishers) Ltd for *The Mother* from *Blade Among the Boys*; to John Farquharson Ltd for *The Green Years* from *Tell Freedom*; to William Collins, Sons & Co Ltd for *The Night of Kondén Diara* from *The Dark Child*; and to Mr Can Themba and the Faith Press for a short passage from the introduction to *Darkness and Light*.

Also special thanks to Ursula and Gilbert Reines for assistance in this anthology.

INTRODUCTION

IT was with a good deal of enthusiasm, coupled with slight trepidation, that I accepted an offer to compile an anthology of contemporary African prose writing for schools and student use within the continent. My only experience, before this, had been the compilation and editing of an anthology of South African writing, *Quartet*, but the task of extending the field to embrace the whole of the English-speaking continent seemed formidable. Also, never to my knowledge had this been done before. More localized anthologies, it is true, had been produced, like *West African Narrative* by Paul Edwards and *Short Stories by South African Writers* by Wright, but an anthology attempting to embrace a much wider field, and intended primarily for school and student use, was another matter. In 1958 we had Peggy Rutherfoord's *Darkness and Light*, and in 1960 Langston Hughes' *African Treasury*, but these were intended primarily for adult reading.

After years of teaching English literature in Cape Town at a High School level, I had become convinced that, important as Shakespeare, Dickens and Sir Walter Scott are, students needed something much more recognizable and immediate in addition (not instead of), in order to synthesize their literary experiences. I would consider it foolhardy to assert that all writers not produced out of the African experience are unacceptable, in favour of local material. As the distinguished writer and critic, Ezekiel Mphahlele clearly states in his *African Image*: 'I have seen

too much that is good in Western culture – for example
its music, literature and theatre – to want to repudiate it.'
I appreciate that my own experience as well as that of my
students would be the poorer for not having been acquainted with the magic of Arden or Wordsworth's
countryside. But I feel this is the isolation of African literature even from the African himself. We had almost reached
a situation whereby the only criterion was always geo-
graphically beyond our province, where novels set outside
the African continent were the only ones justified, and
those set in the continent had to be seen through the eyes of
the European observer, no matter how bigoted, mawkish
and sentimental he was.

An argument has always been that the quality and
quantity of available local material could not
warrant sufficient interest in a teaching anthology. It is my
sincere hope that *Modern African Prose* will at least show this
pessimism to be unfounded, and if the African reaction
should be the rage of Caliban seeing his own reflection,
let him at least see his own reflection and be able to say,
or rather assert, 'this island's mine'.

Of course it is possible to indulge in a long polemic on
what exactly African literature is. This to a certain extent
is what happened (if report proved true), at the first All-
African Writers Conference in Kampala in 1962. Theories
are bound to be tendered ranging from the common unity
of the African experience against neo-colonialism to the
existence of an African personality. Valid or invalid as
these may be, I should like to make it clear that I am here
using the term 'African' in its broadest sense. By African
literature, for the purpose of this anthology, I mean literature produced by Africans (regardless of colour, language
or national distinction), which deals with situations and
experiences happening in the continent. I have therefore
included the work of two white writers from South Africa

as I feel that they must not be denied a place in the body
of African literature. It is impossible to speak of African
literature without recognizing Afrikaans writing in South
Africa, Portuguese poetry in Mozambique or Arabic verse
in the Sudan. Literature, when valid, belongs to all of
human experience and cannot be confined within the
rigid and narrow framework of political and national
prejudice. I, too, have seen too much that is good in
literature produced by Afrikaners in South Africa for us
to deny its existence and importance simply because the
language used is that of an unpopular régime. And I have
also experienced examples of literature by black writers
which I feel has only seen the light of day because of
sociological and anthropological reasons and not because
of literary merit. This is a sign of privileged-class
curiosity or racial patronage which in the final an-
alysis spring from an inverted racialism, with all that
that implies.

This is basically an anthology of contemporary writing
by Africans in English, intended for use in schools and by
students. Of the excerpts from novels and short stories
chosen, eight are from South Africa, eight from West
Africa (four from Nigeria, two from Sierra Leone and one
each from Ghana and Guinea), three from East Africa (two
from Kenya and one from Mozambique). In arriving at
this arrangement I have taken into consideration all of contemporary South African Literature in English regardless
of the racial origin of the writer, and because of this the
volume alone of South African writing is, comparatively,
very large. Also the tradition, in that country, of literature
in English, is very much longer than anywhere else on the
continent, dating back well before the publication of Olive
Schreiner's *Story of an African Farm* in 1883. Nigerian prose
literature in English is being established with writers like

Chinua Achebe and others in this anthology. Sierra Leone has produced Abioseh Nicol and William Conton.

Although this is primarily an anthology of contemporary prose by Africans in English, I feel that you will forgive me for having included French-speaking Camara Laye from Guinea whose books are almost as well known in their English translations as in the original French. I would have liked to have included translations from the writing of Mongo Beti and Ferdinand Oyono, but space alone ruled against this. Sufficient to say that I hope that Laye's *The Night of Kondén Diara* will sufficiently whet appetites to delve into this stimulating and exciting branch of African literature.

East Africa has only two representatives, but after intensive and extensive travelling through these countries, I was finally convinced that prose writing here is still in its early stages and at the moment tends to be anecdotal and explanatory. The fact that the first All-African writers conference was held in East Africa may prove a strong stimulant.

Let me finally state that it is my sincere hope that *Modern African Prose*, although the first, will by no means prove the last, of many endeavours of this kind, and will play its part in fulfilling a basic need and making African writers known to Africa. We might then reach the position when we can say as Can Themba says in his introduction to *Darkness and Light*:

'This is us: Africa speaking to Africa and to the world. ... You can find us in the mielie fields and in the mines: you can find us in in the shebeens quaffing "Macbeth" brews to the jazz and jive of the cities, or outside the grass huts of our fathers telling tales with the old women. You can see us gaffing each other or breaking suddenly into song and dance; into swear-words, fighting and tears. We are here in the robes of our grandfathers and the tight-trousered dress of the big towns. All this is us.'

London,   RICHARD RIVE
September 1963

PETER ABRAHAMS

PETER ABRAHAMS was born in the Transvaal, South Africa, in 1919. He spent his youth in Elsenberg and then returned to the slum of Vrededorp. Educated at St Peter's, Johannesburg, he started writing poetry, and left for Cape Town. After that he left for England where he became South Africa's most prolific prose writer. He has had many novels published in the United States and Europe. At present he is the editor of *West Indian Economist*.

In his autobiography, *Tell Freedom*, Peter Abrahams tells of his first perceptions and experiences; of his coloured mother and his father who was an Ethiopian. His earliest years were experienced in the slums of Vrededorp in Johannesburg, but on the death of his father he was sent to Elsenberg, to live with his Aunt Liza and Uncle Sam. In this place too were formulated at a tender age his experiences with others, especially other racial groups, being beaten up by White boys and forming a tight friendship with the Zulu boy, Joseph. Very suddenly he was fetched by his brother and sister and taken back to the slums of Johannesburg to be reunited with his ailing mother. His experiences after this were the normal squalid and frustrating ones of boyhood in the slumland: having to steal food, selling wood with Danny, sitting in dingy cinemas with Dinny, helping Aunt Mattie to sell illicit liquor, and being forced to beg by much older boys.

The Green Years

Often, at the smithy, I cleaned Mr Wylie's car during the lunch hour. For this he gave me a shilling at the end of each week. Boeta Dick had raised my wages to three shillings. Thus, I went home with four shillings every Saturday afternoon. Half this sum paid for my food and keep. I took a shilling as pocket-money. The other shilling Aunt Mattie put away for me. Once or twice she had borrowed from my savings. She had always asked first. She had always returned it to my little hoard that she kept in her mattress.

One lunch-time, after I had cleaned his car, Mr Wylie said:

'There are some sandwiches on my desk. Take them.'

He drove off. I went to the office. The short-sighted Jewish girl was in her corner, eating her lunch and reading. She looked up.

'Mr Wylie said I can have that.' I pointed.

'All right.'

I took the little package and turned to the door.

'Lee.'

I stopped and turned to her.

'That is your name, isn't it?'

'Yes, missus.'

'Miss, not missus. You only say missus to a married woman.'

Her smile encouraged me.

'We say it to all white women.'

'Then you are wrong. Say miss.'

'Yes, miss.'

'That's better. . . . Tell me, how old are you?'

'Going on for eleven, miss.'

'Why don't you go to school?'

'I don't know, miss.'

'Don't you want to?'

'I don't know, miss.'

'Can you read or write?'

'No, miss.'

'Stop saying miss now.'

'Yes, miss.'

She laughed.

'Sit down. Eat your sandwiches if you like.'

I sat on the edge of the chair near the door.

'So you can't read?'

'No, miss.'

'Wouldn't you like to?'

'I don't know, miss.'

'Want to find out?'

'Yes, miss.'

She turned the pages of the book in front of her. She looked at me, then began to read from *Lamb's Tales from Shakespeare*.

The story of Othello jumped at me and invaded my heart and mind as the young woman read. I was transported to the land where the brave Moor lived and loved and destroyed his love.

The young woman finished.

'Like it?'

'Oh yes!'

'Good. This book is full of stories like that. If you go to school you'll be able to read them for yourself.'

'But can I find a book like that?'

'Yes. There are many books.'

'The same one with the same story?'

'There are thousands.'

'Exactly like it?'

'Exactly.'

'Then I'm going to school!'

'When?'

'Monday.'

'I've started something!' She laughed. 'But why didn't you go before?'

'Nobody told me.'

'You must have seen other children go to school.'

'Nobody told me about the stories.'

'Oh yes, the stories.'

'When I can read and write I'll make stories like that!'

She smiled, leaned back suddenly and reached for her pen. She opened the book.

'Your surname?'

'Abrahams, miss. Peter is my real name, Peter Abrahams.'

She wrote in the book.

'Here, I've put your name in it. It's for you.'

I looked at her writing.

'That my name?'

'Yes. I've written "this is the property of Peter Abrahams".'

'But which is my name?'

'Those two words.' She pointed. 'Well, take it!'

I took the book. I held it gingerly. I moved to the door, backward. She shook her head and laughed. The laughter ended abruptly.

'Oh God,' she said and shook her head again.

'Thank you, miss. Thank you!'

Her eyes looked strangely bright behind the thick glasses.

'Go away!' she said. 'Go away ... and good luck. ...'

I hesitated awkwardly at the door. Was she crying? And why?

'Yes, thank you, miss. Thank you!'

'You know he will have missed half the lessons, sir. It's middle of term, my class is overflowing, and he's big and old enough to be in standard four. . . . Why didn't you come at the start of term?'

'I was working, miss.'

'Now look here! Do I really have to tell you, a coloured teacher, that education is only compulsory for whites and no one cares whether this boy goes to school or not? Do I have to read you the illiteracy figures among your own people? You're coloured, I'm not: do I have to tell *you* about the condition of your people and your children?'

'No, sir. . . . But —'

'I know, Sarah. Your class is three times as big as it should be; you haven't slates or pencils for all of them; some are so big they're ready to have babies or grow beards; you haven't enough benches; you can't control them. I know all that. But set this against it. A boy at work hears a story and the story makes him come here. He says "Please, I want to learn". Are we to turn him away because he hasn't observed all the rules? Is your community so rich that it can afford to do that? . . . Listen! I've an idea. We'll press these big ones. We'll make them do the work of three days in one. . . . Boy! Peter!'

'Sir?'

'Afraid of hard work?'

'No, sir.'

'All right! I'll make you work. I promise you'll read and write by the end of this year. The rules will be hard. If there is any trouble or slackness I want the teacher to send you to me and I shall use the cane, hard. All right?'

'Yes, sir.'

'See, Sarah. The boy and I are in a hurry. Help us. We haven't much time. . . . Take him away!'

'Yes, sir.'

'Hello, Sarah! Another?'

'Yes. He and Visser are in a hurry. Visser's thinking up

a new scheme for making the big ones do the work of three years in one.'

'Oh, my God!'

'It's killing.'

'One thing to be said for the old boy. He's interested in coloured education, and he's the only Principal about whom I can say that in all the years I've been here. And a *Boer*! You know he's been in an asylum.'

'Yes. Mad Boer poet. Easy enough for him to sit at his desk thinking up beautiful schemes. We have to do all the dirty work.'

'Cheer up, girl. He's not so bad. I must go'n silence my screaming brats. See you.'

'Come.'

'All right. You may sit down. This is our new boy, Peter Abrahams. Make room for him in the corner at the back, Adams.'

'Please, miss . . .'

'Yes?'

'There is no room. We're so tight we can hardly move our arms to write.'

'Peter must have a place. Make room as best you can.'

'Yes, miss.'

'Now! Put up your hands those of you who have whole slates. Not one?'

'They're all cracked, miss.'

'It doesn't matter if they are cracked. Up now . . . One . . . Two. Only three?'

'Mine is my own, miss.'

'What you mean, Margaret, is that it is one you bought and not one supplied by the school.'

'Yes, miss.'

'Then say what you mean. All right, you may put down your hand, Margaret.'

'Please, miss . . .'

'Yes, Thomas?'

'My slate is cracked across the middle. I can let him . . .'

'Peter.'

'That is very good of you, Thomas. Thank you. But isn't that where Jones sits? He'll be back tomorrow and want his seat.'

'He's not coming back, miss. His father's gone to jail so he must go to work to help his mother.'

'Are you sure of this?'

'Yes, miss.'

'It's a shame. You liked Jones so much, didn't you, miss?'

'That's enough out of you, Adams. Thank you, Thomas.'

'Is your father alive, Peter?'

'No, miss.'

'Then things are not too easy?'

'No, miss.'

'Take this card. You'll see children standing in a line during the lunch break. Join them and show this and you'll get a free lunch. That's all. You can go to your place.'

'Thank you, miss. I'm sorry to make more work for you.'

'Come back here, Peter. . . . I don't want you to think any more about making work for me or anybody. Understand?'

'Yes, miss.'

'We are here to teach and help you. I'm sorry I made you think that. You've often said something you don't mean, haven't you?'

'Yes, miss.'

'Well, it was the same. Don't think about it. And don't repeat what you heard me and the other teacher say about the Principal.'

'Yes, miss.'

.   .   .   .   .

A   B   C   D   E   F   G,
H   I   J   K   L   M   N,
O   P   Q   R   S   T   U,
V   W   X   Y   Z makes the Alpha-bet.

Two times one are two,
Two times two are four – old woman scrubs the floor.
Two times three are six – the hen has many chicks.
Two times four are eight – for school I won't be late.
Two times seven are fourteen – haven't a thought in.
Two times nine are eighteen – oh golly!
Two times ten are twenty – these sums are very plenty!

C is a letter in the alphabet,
A is a letter in the alphabet,
T is a letter in the alphabet:
Put them together and you have a cat.

'Please, miss . . .'
'Yes?'
'Are all the books in the world made from the alphabet?'
'Yes, all the books in the world are made from the alphabet.'
'Jee-zus!'
'What?'
'Nothing, miss; thank you.'
'Hey! Look at the new one among our hungry lot. He's in our class. Peter Abrahams. Hey! Peter Abrahams! Like lining up with the other cattle for a bit of bread and dirty cocoa? They spit in the cocoa!'
'Ha! ha! ha! ha!'

'Shhh! Old Visser's heard you!'
'Hey! No use running away, you little coward! I know you! Come here!'
'Sir?'

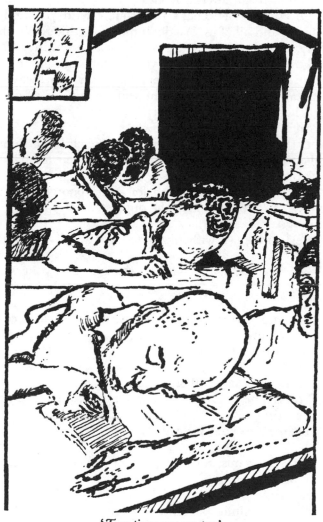

'*Two times one are two*'

'I heard what you said. I've a good mind to expel you!'

'Didn't mean anything, sir.'

'Of course not! That's the trouble with you and this country and all of us. We don't mean anything. We abuse, deny, outrage, insult, and don't mean anything. You're looked down upon. Have you learnt nothing from it? Must you look down on someone else? Go away! If I hear any more remarks from you or anyone else . . . . Teacher!'

'Sir?'

'Is there no way we can protect these children from the vulgar remarks of others while they get their food?'

'No, sir.'

'They're being humiliated for being poorer than their fellows. Snobbery among the oppressed!'

'Let's not play with him. He's got woolly hair like a *kaffir*.'

'Go to hell! Yours may be straight but your skin is black!'

'. . . And that is the story of Joseph, who had a coat of many colours.'

'Is it a true story, sir?'

'Yes.'

'Please read us another one, sir.'

'You're one of the three-class students, aren't you?'

'Yes, sir.'

'Then off to your history class. . . .'

'Ah, Abrahams. So you're letting things slip after only six months.'

'No, sir.'

'Are you calling the teacher a liar?'

'No, sir.'

'Are you tired of working hard? Letting me down? None

of the others have, you know. Do you want to do only the ordinary classes?'

'No, sir.'

'You'd better tell me all about it.'

'It's arithmetic, sir.'

'What about it?'

'I can't do it, sir.'

'Have you tried?'

'Yes, sir.'

'Hard?'

'Yes, sir.'

'This record says you show no real interest in it.'

'I've tried, sir.'

'Do you mean the record is untrue?'

'No, sir. I mean I've tried hard to be interested.'

'And failed?'

'Yes, sir.'

'You know, of course, that I don't make the laws about examinations.'

'Yes, sir.'

'Well, unless you get a certain average for arithmetic your very high average in all the other subjects won't help you. That is the law, and I didn't make it. I want to push you through as fast as I can but you must work at arithmetic. Relax a little with the other subjects, if you like.'

'I like the other subjects, sir.'

'I know. But to get where you want to go you can't only do what you like. . . Where do you want to go? What do you want to do?'

'Those stories, sir.'

'In the book the young woman gave you?'

'Yes, sir.'

'I was wondering whether you had begun to forget them.'

'I'm trying to read it now, sir.'

'Getting anything out of it?'

'A little.'

'Well, there you have it. Between you and the further knowledge that would help you get everything out of that book, stands arithmetic. It's like a lion barring your road. You either turn back because you cannot cope with it, or you kill it, and go on. There is no other way. The makers of our educational laws have not provided for poets. I want you to kill that lion and go on. Arithmetic is silly in a poet's armoury but you must master it and get that average. . . . I promised you my cane if you were ever sent to me. We must keep our promises. Let down your trousers, then go back and let the sting of the cane help you kill the lion. . . .'

'But if the earth is round, sir, why don't things fall off it? Why don't people and things and the seas fall off it?'

'Because, my dear Arendse, it has a gravitational pull which prevents all these things happening.'

'Then, sir, will you please explain this pull thing to us?'

'Yes, sir.'

'Please . . .'

'Oh, my aunt! Do you, Arendse, and all the others, do you realize that there is a strict set scheme for each class? Certain things are taught in standard one, certain things in standard two and so on. Gravity and science are things you shouldn't know anything about till next year.'

'But, sir . . .'

'Well?'

'That means that till next year we've just got to accept your word about everything you say about the earth. And for a year we'll go on wanting to know how things stick to the earth if it is round.'

'And you know Mr Visser told us always to ask if things didn't seem very clear to us.'

'All right! Sit down, Flora, and you, Arendse. Mr Visser's specials! . . . But before I go on to gravity, Peter's been snapping his fingers. What is it you want to know, Mr Abrahams?'

'When you talked about how to prove the earth is round, sir, you said the curve of the land was sure proof. But the land is full of hills and valleys; so how can one see this curve? And none of us have been to sea, so we don't know whether it does curve. So you see, sir, if you answer Arendse's question before proving the earth is round it will be hard to believe in this pull, because you won't need it on a flat earth.'

'You are the original flat-earthers. Now listen! . . .'

'Hello, Peter.'

'Hello, Ellen.'

'Walk with me to the end of the playground.'

'I can't.'

'Please . . . Or don't you want to?'

'I want to but I can't.'

'Why not?'

'Why do you ask me when you know I have to line up?'

'Please don't be angry.'

'Then don't ask when you know the answer.'

'I only asked because you don't have to line up.'

'I want to eat.'

'I brought an extra lunch.'

'For me?'

'Yes.'

'Why?'

'I like you. You're the best boy in Visser's special.'

'Arendse gets better marks.'

'Only in the things you don't like.'

'His average is better.'

'I heard a teacher say your intelligence was better. And I agree. Come. I'm shy. I don't want to give you your lunch where everybody can see.'

'I thought you were poorer than me. You are thinner.'

'We're poor in everything except food. My ma works where they waste a lot of food and she brings a lot of it home. There's chicken in your sandwiches. I can't get fat no matter how much I eat. Suppose I'd better tell you I've got a bad chest.'

'Why?'

'Here, take your sandwiches. We're far away from the others now. Let's go'n sit under that tree . . . Nice?'

'Hmmm.'

'I'm glad. I'll bring you all the nicest things. I've some sweets for after.'

'I've nothing to give you.'

'I don't want anything. I just want you to be my boy if you like me. That's why I told you about my chest. My granny says one must always tell the truth. But even if you don't like me, I will still bring your lunch every day. What I mean is every day as long as my ma stays with us. She may go away and then there won't be any more food. . . . Do you like me?'

'Yes.'

'Really? Cross your heart?'

'Cross my heart.'

'I thought you did, but I wasn't sure. But I knew you'd never tell me if I didn't ask you. And it's not easy for a girl to tell a boy she likes him.'

'It's not easy for a boy.'

'Not if he's like you. . . . Have some of mine, please. I can't eat all of it. And a man must eat more than a woman. I told my granny all about you. She wants me to bring you home. But you must not come if you don't want to.'

'I want to! I'll carry your books this afternoon.'

'Good. Oh, I'm so glad you won't be in the line-up again. It made me want to cry when I heard them say things.'

'Wish I could give you something. Here, I've a top and some marbles.'

'Keep them. . . Just be my boy.'

'I am your boy and I think you're the nicest girl in the school.'

'I'm dark and I have kinky hair.'

'Who cares? I like you!'

'I want you to top the class for me!'

'No. You must be first. That's what I want. Will you?'

'I'll try if that's what you really want.'

'You'll be first, I'll be second and old Arendse third. I want to be proud of my girl.'

'All right! I'll do it. . . . There's the bell. Golly, we'll have to run. We'll be late.'

'Give me your hand.'

'Not too fast, please. It'll make me cough.'

'Old Visser's proud of his specials, Sarah. Nearly a dozen of them have passed the standard two exam. The first five topped even the regular standard two class. Makes one feel the awful grind was worth while.'

'Yes, he is good. . . . What is it, Peter?'

'Mr Visser said you might like to see the prize he gave me for my essay.'

'Oh . . . Let me see. I didn't know there was a prize for an essay . . . *Poems of John Keats*. . . . But you can't read this yet.'

'He told me to tell you I couldn't read *Lamb's Tales* once and that brought me here.'

'The old devil! And I just had nice thoughts about him.'

'He wants you to read the Everyman text to me.'

'Here it is: "Everyman, I will go with thee and be thy guide in thy most need to go by thy side.' Does it mean anything to you?'

'No, miss. But Mr Visser said I should say it will one day.'

'The old devil! And they thought him too mad for a white school . . .! Run along, Peter.'

NOTES

Mr Wylie : owner of a smithy in Vrededorp, Johannesburg
Boeta Dick : Peter's immediate superior at the smithy
Aunt Mattie : his relation with whom he is staying
Boer : white, Afrikaans-speaking South African
Kaffir : contemptuous term for an African

OTHER BOOKS BY PETER ABRAHAMS

Dark Testament (Allen & Unwin, 1942)
Song of the City (D. Crisp, 1945)
Mine Boy (D. Crisp, 1946; Faber & Faber, 1954)
Wild Conquest (Faber & Faber, 1951)
Path of Thunder (Faber & Faber, 1952)
Return to Goli (Faber & Faber, 1953)
A Wreath for Udomo (Allen & Unwin, 1956)
Jamaica (H.M.S.O., 1957)
A Night of Their Own (Faber & Faber, 1965)

CHINUA ACHEBE

CHINUA ACHEBE was born in Ogidi, Eastern Nigeria, in 1930. He was educated at Government College, Umuahia, and at University College, Ibadan, now the University of Ibadan. He has held many important posts in the Nigerian Broadcasting Corporation and is now the Director of its External Service. His first novel, *Things Fall Apart*, was published in 1958 and won the Margaret Wrong Prize. *No Longer at Ease* was published in 1960 and won the Nigerian National Trophy. His third novel, *Arrow of God*, was published this year and enthusiastically received.

The novel from which this excerpt is taken, *No Longer at Ease*, tells of Obi Okonkwo, a young Eastern Nigerian, a promising representative of his generation, the bright boy of his village, who returns from his studies in England required to live up to the expectations of his family and tribe, and at the same time to breathe the heady atmosphere of Lagos. As a civil servant Obi holds a respectable job; as the fiancé of Clara, the girl he met on the boat, he has much to look forward to; yet he falls victim to the corruption of the capital. Clara turns out to be *Osu*, an outcast, one dedicated to the gods. This excerpt tells of his meeting with his father when the matter of his marriage to an *osu* is broached.

B

Father and Son

Obi's serious talks with his father began after the family had prayed and all but the two of them had gone to bed. The prayers had taken place in mother's room because she was again feeling very weak, and whenever she was unable to join the others in the parlour her husband conducted prayers in her room.

The devil and his works featured prominently in that night's prayers. Obi had a shrewd suspicion that his affair with Clara was one of the works. But it was only a suspicion; there was nothing yet to show that his parents had actually heard of it.

Mr Okonkwo's easy capitulation in the afternoon on the matter of heathen singing was quite clearly a tactical move. He let the enemy gain ground in a minor skirmish while he prepared his forces for a great offensive.

He said to Obi after prayers: 'I know you must be tired after the great distance you have travelled. There is something important we must talk about, but it can wait until tomorrow, till you have had time to rest.'

'We can talk now,' said Obi. 'I am not too tired. We get used to driving long distances.'

'Come to my room, then,' said his father, leading the way with the ancient hurricane lamp. There was a small table in the middle of the room. Obi remembered when it was bought. Carpenter Moses had built it and offered it to the church at harvest. It was put up for auction after the Harvest Service and sold. He could not now remember how much his father had paid for it, eleven and threepence perhaps.

'I don't think there is kerosene in this lamp,' said his father, shaking the lamp near his ear. It sounded quite

empty. He brought half a bottle of kerosene from his cupboard and poured a little into the lamp. His hands were
no longer steady and he spilt some of the kerosene. Obi
did not offer to do it for him because he knew his father
would never dream of letting children pour kerosene into
his lamp; they would not know how to do it properly.

'How were all our people in Lagos when you left them?'
he asked. He sat on his wooden bed while Obi sat on a low
stool facing him, drawing lines with his finger on the
dusty top of the Harvest table.

'Lagos is a very big place. You can travel the distance
from here to Abame and still be in Lagos.'

'So they said. But you have a meeting of Umuofia
people?' It was half-question, half-statement.

'Yes we have a meeting. But it is only once a month.'
And he added: 'It is not always that one finds time to
attend.' The fact was he had not attended since November.

'True,' said his father. 'But in a strange land one should
always move near one's kinsmen.' Obi was silent, signing
his name in the dust on the table. 'You wrote to me some
time ago about a girl you had seen. How does the matter
stand now?'

'That is one reason why I came. I want us to go and
meet her people and start negotiations. I have no money
now, but at least we can begin to talk.' Obi had decided
that it would be fatal to sound apologetic or hesitant.

'Yes,' said his father. 'That is the best way.' He thought
a little and again said yes, it was the best way. Then a
new thought seemed to occur to him. 'Do we know who
his girl is and where she comes from?' Obi hesitated just
enough for his father to ask the question again in a
different way. 'What is her name?'

'She is the daughter of Okeke, a native of Mbaino.'

'Which Okeke? I know about three. One is a retired
teacher, but it would not be that one.'

'That is the one,' said Obi.

'Josiah Okeke?'

Obi said yes, that was his name.

His father laughed. It was the kind of laughter one sometimes heard from a masked ancestral spirit. He would salute you by name and ask you if you knew who he was. You would reply with one hand humbly touching the ground that you did not, that he was beyond human knowledge. Then he might laugh as if through a throat of metal. And the meaning of that laughter was clear: 'I did not really think you would know, you miserable worm!'

Obi's father's laughter vanished as it had come – without warning, leaving no footprints.

'You cannot marry the girl,' he said quite simply.

'Eh?'

'I said you cannot marry the girl.'

'But why, Father?'

'Why? I shall tell you why. But first tell me this. Did you find out or try to find out anything about this girl?'

'Yes.'

'What did you find out?'

'That they are osu.'

'You mean to tell me that you knew, and you ask me why?'

'I don't think it matters. We are Christians.' This had some effect, nothing startling though. Only a little pause and a slightly softer tone.

'We are Christians,' he said. 'But that is no reason to marry an osu.'

'The Bible says that in Christ there are no bond or free.'

'My son,' said Okonkwo, 'I understand what you say. But this thing is deeper than you think.'

'What is this thing? Our fathers in their darkness and ignorance called an innocent man osu, a thing given to idols, and thereafter he became an outcast, and his children, and his children's children for ever. But have we not seen the light of the Gospel?' Obi used the very words that his father might have used in talking to his heathen kinsmen.

There was a long silence. The lamp was now burning too brightly. Obi's father turned down the wick a little and then resumed his silence. After what seemed ages he said: 'I know Josiah Okeke very well.' He was looking steadily in front of him. His voice sounded tired: 'I know him and I know his wife. He is a good man and a great Christian. But he is osu. Naaman, captain of the host of Syria, was a great man and honourable, he was also a mighty man of valour, but he was a leper.' He paused so that his great and felicitous analogy might sink in with all its heavy and dreadful weight.

'Osu is like leprosy in the minds of our people. I beg of you, my son, not to bring the mark of shame and of leprosy into your family. If you do, your children and your children's children unto the third and fourth genera-tions will curse your memory. It is not for myself I speak; my days are few. You will bring sorrow on your head and on the heads of your children. Who will marry your daughters? Whose daughters will your sons marry? Think of that, my son. We are Christians, but we cannot marry our own daughters.'

'But all that is going to change. In ten years things will be quite different from what they are now.'

The old man shook his head sadly but said no more. Obi repeated his points. What made an osu different from other men and women? Nothing but the ignorance of their forefathers. Why should they, who had seen the light of the Gospel, remain in that ignorance?

He slept very little that night. His father had not appeared as difficult as he had expected. He had not been won over yet, but he had clearly weakened. Obi felt strangely happy and excited. He had not been through

anything quite like this before. He was used to speaking to
his mother like an equal, even from his childhood, but his
father had always been different. He was not exactly
remote from his family, but there was something about
him that made one think of the patriarchs, those giants
hewn from granite. Obi's strange happiness sprang not
only from the little ground he had won on the argument,
but from the direct human contact he had made with his
father for the first time in his twenty-six years.

As soon as he woke up in the morning he went to see
his mother. It was six o'clock by his watch, but still very
dark. He groped his way to her room. She was awake, for
she asked who it was as soon as he entered the room. He
went and sat on her bed and felt her temperature with his
palm. She had not slept much on account of the pain
in her stomach. She said she had now lost faith in
the European medicine and would like to try a native
doctor.

At that moment Obi's father rang his little bell to
summon the family to morning prayers. He was surprised
when he came in with the lamp and saw Obi already there.
Eunice came in wrapped up in her loin-cloth. She was
the last of the children and the only one at home. That
was what the world had come to. Children left their old
parents at home and scattered in all directions in search
of money. It was hard on an old woman with eight
children. It was like having a river and yet washing one's
hands with spittle.

Behind Eunice came Joy and Mercy, distant relations
who had been sent by their parents to be trained in house-
keeping by Mrs Okonkwo.

Afterwards, when they were alone again, she listened
silently and patiently to the end. Then she raised herself
up and said: 'I dreamt a bad dream, and I felt something
creepy against my skin. I looked down on the bed and
found that a swarm of white termites had eaten it up, and

the mat and the white cloth. Yes, termites had eaten up the bed right under me.'

A strange feeling like cold dew descended on Obi's head.

'I did not tell anybody about that dream in the morning. I carried it in my heart wondering what it was. I took down my Bible and read the portion for the day. It gave me some strength, but my heart was still not at rest. In the afternoon your father came in with a letter from Joseph to tell us that you were going to marry an osu. I saw the meaning of my death in the dream. Then I told your father about it.' She stopped and took a deep breath. 'I have nothing to tell you in this matter except one thing. If you want to marry this girl, you must wait until I am no more. If God hears my prayers, you will not wait long.' She stopped again. Obi was terrified by the change that had come over her. She looked strange as if she had suddenly gone off her head.

'Mother!' he called, as if she was going away. She held up her hand for silence.

'But if you do the thing while I am alive, you will have my blood on your head, because I shall kill myself.' She sank down completely exhausted.

Obi kept to his room throughout that day. Occasionally he fell asleep for a few minutes. Then he would be woken up by the voices of neighbours and acquaintances who came to see him. But he refused to see anybody. He told Eunice to say that he was unwell from long travelling. He knew that it was a particularly bad excuse. If he was unwell, then surely that was all the more reason why he should be seen. Anyway he refused to be seen, and the neighbours and acquaintances felt wounded. Some of them spoke their mind there and then, others managed to sound as if nothing had happened. One old woman even prescribed a cure for the illness, even though *she* had not seen the patient. Long journeys, she said, were very troublesome. The thing to do was to take strong purgative medicine to wash out all the odds and ends in the belly.

Obi did not appear for evening prayers. He heard his father's voice as if from a great distance, going on for a very long time. Whenever it appeared to have finished, his voice rose again. At last Obi heard several voices saying the Lord's Prayer. But everything sounded far away, as voices and the cries of insects sound to a man in a fever.

His father came into his room with his hurricane lamp and asked how he felt. Then he sat down on the only chair in the room, took up his lamp again and shook it for kerosene. It sounded satisfactory and he turned the wick down, until the flame was practically swallowed up in the lamp's belly. Obi lay perfectly still on his back, looking up at the bamboo ceiling, the way he had been told as a child not to sleep. For it was said if he slept on his back and a spider crossed the ceiling above him he would have bad dreams.

He was amazed at the irrelevant thoughts that passed through his mind at this the greatest crisis in his life. He waited for his father to speak that he might put up another fight to justify himself. His mind was troubled not only by what had happened but also by the discovery that there was nothing in him with which to challenge it honestly. All day he had striven to rouse his anger and his conviction, but he was honest enough with himself to realize that the response he got, no matter how violent it sometimes appeared, was not genuine. It came from the periphery, and not the centre, like the jerk in the leg of the dead frog when a current is applied to it. But he could not accept the present state of his mind as final, so he searched desperately for something that would trigger off the inevitable reaction. Perhaps another argument with his father, more violent than the first; for it was true what the Ibos say, that when a coward sees a man he can beat he becomes hungry for a fight. He had discovered he could beat his father.

But Obi's father sat in silence, declining to fight. Obi turned on his side and drew a deep breath. But still his father said nothing.

'I shall return to Lagos the day after tomorrow,' Obi said finally.

'Did you not say you had a week to spend with us?'

'Yes, but I think it will be better if I return earlier.'

After this there was another long silence. Then his father spoke, but not about the thing that was on their minds. He began slowly and quietly, so quietly that his words were barely audible. It seemed as if he was not really speaking to Obi. His face was turned sideways so that Obi saw it in vague profile.

'I was more than a boy when I left my father's house and went with the missionaries. He placed a curse on me. I was not there but my brothers told me it was true. When a man curses his own child it is a terrible thing. And I was his first son.'

Obi had never heard about the curse. In broad daylight and in happier circumstances he would not have attached any importance to it. But that night he felt strangely moved with pity for his father.

'When they brought me word that he had hanged himself I told them that those who live by the sword must perish by the sword. Mr Braddeley, the white man who was our teacher, said it was not the right thing to say and told me to go home for the burial. I refused to go. Mr Braddeley thought I spoke about the white man's messenger whom my father had killed. He did not know I spoke about Ikemefuna with whom I grew up in my mother's hut until the day came when my father killed him with his own hands.' He paused to collect his thoughts, turned in his chair and faced the bed on which Obi lay. 'I tell you all this so that you may know what it was in those days to become a Christian. Because I suffered I understand Christianity – more than you will ever do.' He stopped rather abruptly. Obi thought it was a pause, but he had finished.

Obi knew the sad story of Ikemefuna who was given to Umuofia by her neighbours in appeasement. Obi's father and Ikemefuna became inseparable. But one day the Oracle of the Hills and the Caves decreed that the boy should be killed. Obi's grandfather loved the boy. But when the moment came it was his matchet that cut him down. Even in those days some elders said it was a great wrong that a man should raise his hands against a child that called him father.

OTHER BOOKS BY CHINUA ACHEBE

Things Fall Apart (Heinemann, 1958)
No Longer at Ease (Heinemann, 1960)
Arrow of God (Heinemann, 1964)
A Man of the People (Heinemann, 1966)

EZEKIEL MPHAHLELE

EZEKIEL MPHAHLELE was born in 1919 in the slums of
Pretoria. He was thirteen before he could attend a school. His
childhood was spent carrying washing which his mother did
for the white residents so that her three children might eat
and gain an education. Despite all handicaps he completed
High School and went on to become a teacher of English and
Afrikaans. Dismissed from school for his opposition to Bantu
Education, he became the fiction editor of *Drum* magazine in
Johannesburg. He finally qualified as an M.A. with distinction.
He went into exile in Nigeria where he taught and lectured at
the University of Ibadan and then went to Paris as head of the
African Department of the Congress for Cultural Freedom. He
is now Director of Chemchemi in Nairobi.

In his autobiography, *Down Second Avenue*, from which this
excerpt is taken, Ezekiel Mphahlele looks back on his years in
the Reserves. His mother's sudden appearance one day changed
the course of things for him and, at thirteen, his life re-started
in Pretoria. Here things were, if anything, much worse; a
drunken father violent towards his mother, the children being
handed over to their grandmother, the father finally in prison
and the mother in hospital. Here life started in Second Avenue
with grandmother and her daughter, Aunt Dora, who earned
their living by brewing illicit liquor and taking in white
people's washing. Somehow he managed to be put through
primary school and finally he went to St Peter's in Johannesburg. From there he went on to Adams College where he
qualified as a teacher. His career was shortlived and he was
put out of his job for his opposition to Bantu Education. Life

became extremely difficult for him and finally, having become
a graduate and, therefore, employable elsewhere, he left South
Africa to teach in Nigeria.

This excerpt shows life for Zeke at the tender age of thirteen
in Second Avenue, and is especially a portrayal of the people
who had a permanent effect on his later life.

The Location

We were getting used to Second Avenue life, my brother,
sister and I. Avenues and streets were new to us. Now,
why would people go and build houses all in a straight
line? Why would people go to a bucket in a small building
to relieve themselves?

Why would people want to be cut off from one another
by putting up fences? It wasn't so at Maupaneng. Houses
didn't stand in any order and we visited one another and
could sit round the communal fire and tell one another
stories until the cocks crowed. Not in Second Avenue. And
yet, although people didn't seem to be interested in one
another, they spoke with a subtle unity of voice. They
still behaved as a community.

My grandmother was head of a large family. She was
a Mopedi, whose father had also been a Mphahlele, but
no blood-relation of my father's. So many people were
surnamed Mphahlele that Chief Mphahlele decreed that
everyone but those of his family should look for a new
surname, because, in any case, the name didn't neces-
sarily signify blood-relationship. But then several had gone
to the cities, and he gave it up. Grandmother had been
married to Titus Mogale, a Mopedi of Sekhukhuniland in
the Lydenburg district. Both of them were but children
when the white 'Filibusters', led by Captain Ritter, were
trying to dislodge King Sekhukhuni from his mountains.

Grandmother told me how the Bapedi had always hated the Swazis, down to this day, because when the 'Filibusters' had failed to capture the King of the Bapedi, Ritter had organized bloodthirsty Swazis, who subsequently wormed their way through and slaughtered every man, woman and child in the hills and captured the King.

My mother, Aunt Dora and three uncles were born in the district of Eastern Transvaal. Aunt Dora, her three children and the three uncles lived with us. And we had two rooms. Both were bedrooms and the room which had a table and four chairs was bedroom and sitting-room. We cooked on the back veranda. Granny leased three rooms. My mother, eldest in the family, worked in one of the suburbs as a domestic servant and lived in. She came to see us one Sunday in a fortnight.

Here the young men who migrate to the cities to work still fight as they did on moonlight nights in the country. And so every Sunday afternoon they march with big broad slabs of human flesh they call feet to some place outside the city. They moved in rival teams. In Pretoria these 'Malaita' were provided with a piece of ground and they marched under police guard. In this way, the 'natives let off steam', as the Pretoria City Council said.

Our house faced Barber Street. It was a family re-creation to sit on the veranda on Sunday afternoons. The malaita beat on the tar with their large feet past our house; the police dispersed in front of our house before going each to his beat; visiting domestic workers from the suburbs passed our house before they swept into the location, and passed in front of our house again on their way out. It was a common Sunday afternoon spectacle for a policeman to pass in front of our house propelling a man by the scruff of the neck to the police station. Women particularly fascinated us in their various styles of dress. Some hobbled past in awkward high heels, evidently feeling the pinch; others were really smart and enviable.

Our fence needed constant pulling up because it was always falling. Grandmother said how she wanted to plant flowers. We tried valiantly, but none of us had the guts to fetch water for the plants. We gave it up. The best we ever got to doing was set up a grape-vine creeper which made pleasant shade for the family to do washing. The rusty iron gate was a particular nuisance. The ants kept eating up the standards underneath, and we kept digging in the poles until we, the gate and everything else about it resigned ourselves to an acute angle and we piled stones around the standards to maintain the *status quo*. We swept the yard, however, a ten-foot border on all sides of the corrugated walls. The women made a lovely path from the gate to the front door, branching off to the back of the house. This was skirted on either side by small mud walls, and the floor was paved with mud smoothed with a slippery stone and then smeared with dung. Small pebbles had been worked in in repeated triangular patterns. A small wall separated this path from our ash dump, where we constantly scratched for coke to use again in our braziers. The ash we then poured into the garbage can. Towards the front of our yard, facing Barber Street and Second Avenue, we often planted maize. From this patch we harvested exactly seven cobs most years. We, the smaller members of the family, netted half a cob each. Our backyard was fenced with a four-foot mud wall. The floor of the yard was paved with mud because that was where we cooked – we and the tenants in the two back rooms. These rooms, together with our passage that ran from the back to the front doors, opened on to a small veranda. This we used as a kitchen in the winter. Our kitchen table stood at a corner, for as long as I can remember, where we had found it when we came from Pietersburg. The floor of this porch, not more than six feet deep, was laid in broken uneven slabs of slate. No matter how hard we scrubbed the slabs, there

were always spots of candle wax which stuck out like
carbuncles.

At another corner Mathebula kept his blankets and the
sack on which he slept on a soap-box. He slept in the
porch. He was a witch-doctor and had dropped in one
day to ask for shelter. It turned out that he had come
from Shanganaland in the north and was homeless.
Grandmother had kept him. The ash around the fireplace
was a perennial problem. The corrugated-iron walls were
always sooty, except towards the edge of the porch, where
Chipile, the Indian soft-goods hawker, often pencilled his
invoice. At one end of the backyard Mathebula could be
seen any morning sitting on a mat, his bones scattered in
front of him while he mumbled magic words in Shangana.
All of us, visitors alike, tried, as much as room allowed, to
move clear of Mathebula's sphere of influence.

I did most of the domestic work because my sister and
brother were still too small. My uncles were considered
too big. I woke up at 4.30 in the morning to make fire
in a brazier fashioned out of an old lavatory bucket.
I washed, made breakfast coffee for the family and tea
for grandmother as she did not take coffee. 'That's how
I stopped taking coffee', said grandmother, telling us the
story of how, when she was a girl, someone hit her with a
stone and drew blood from the temple. She had picked
up the stone and a witch-doctor had treated it with some
medicine, but this hadn't helped because since then she
was unable to eat beef or drink coffee. They made her so
sick.

After morning coffee, which we often had with mealie-
meal porridge from the previous night's left-overs, we went
to school. Back from school I had to clean the house as
Aunt Dora and Grandmother did the white people's
washing all day. Fire had to be made, meat had to be
bought from an Indian butchery in the Asiatic Reserve.
We were so many in the family that I had to cook porridge

twice in the same big pot. We hardly ever bought more
than a pound of mutton in weight. Weekdays supper was
very simple: just porridge and meat. When there was no
money we fried tomatoes. We never ate vegetables except
on Sundays. We never had butter except when we had
a visitor from Johannesburg. Same with custard. And then
I don't remember ever seeing a pound of butter. We
bought a tickey's – three pence worth – when we did. On
such days we, the children, made a queue to have grandmother smear a sparing layer of butter on one slice only
of the bread.

At breakfast bread was cut up. The grown-ups were
given theirs first in saucers. Then I rationed the remainder
in slices and bits of slices. Our youngest uncle, not much
older than I, picked his first, which was the greatest
quantity. Then I followed, and my brother and then my
sister. We ate supper out of the same plate, we children;
and meat was dished out in varying sizes and the ritual
was repeated. We never sat at table. Only a visitor was
treated to such modern innovations.

On Monday mornings, at about four o'clock, I started
off for the suburbs to fetch washing for Aunt Dora.
Thursday and Friday afternoons I had to take back the
washing. If I was lucky enough I borrowed a bicycle from
a tenant of ours we called simply 'Oompie' – uncle – when
he was not using it on his rounds in the location collecting
numbers from gamblers for the Chinese *fah-fee*. If I
couldn't get the bicycle for the morning or afternoon I
carried the bundles on my head and walked – about
seven miles for a single journey.

Like all other tenants, Oompie sometimes quarrelled
with Grandmother over tidiness. I was sure, then, that I
wasn't going to get the bicycle. When I walked I couldn't
use the pair of tennis shoes I'd been bought for Sunday
wear. Winter mornings were most trying when the air
penetrated the big cracks round the edges of my feet.

When I came back I went to school. I could never do my homework until about ten o'clock at night when I had washed up and everybody else had gone to bed. We all slept in the same room which had boxes of clothing and a kitchen dresser. My aunt and her husband slept in the room which had a table and chairs.

Because we were so many in the family, there was only one bedstead – a three-quarter institution occupied by Grandmother and Aunt Dora's children. The wooden floor of the room we slept in had two large holes. There was always a sharp young draught coming up from underneath the floor. Coupled with this, our heads were a playground for mice, which also did havoc on food and clothing.

Sometimes I stole cooked meat and put it in my pocket. I forgot all about it until I was reminded by a large hole in the pocket where our night visitors had celebrated their jubilee. Early winter mornings a large cold drop of water fell on your cheek or into your ear from the iron roof and you woke up with a start. The only window there was misty because it had been shut all night. You heard the sharp whistle of the regular steam train passing, from Pietersburg. You heard the coal-black Nyasa police corporal yell his drill commands on the police station premises in First Avenue. You also heard his whistle. Soon, you knew, they'd be marching with heavy-booted strides up Barber Street, past our house. Then they'd stop and disperse to yet another yell, and go each to his own beat on the row of Indian and Chinese shops facing the location. They hardly ever entered the location on their regular beats. If all this happened while you were in bed you knew you were late in getting out of the blankets and the rest of the morning was going to be a headlong rush to the accompaniment of Grandmother's mumblings and moanings. You soon learned that it was never wise to leave a window open in Marabastad, even on thick mothy summer nights. We were always scared of burglars and what Grandmother called 'wicked night prowlers who've no respect for creatures made in the image of God'. These were witches. There was also the rain to keep out. Summer and autumn bring heavy rains over Pretoria.

I can never remember Marabastad in the rainy summer months. It always comes back to me with its winters. And then I cannot remember ever feeling warm except when I was at the fire or in the sun.

I was cycling one Monday morning from Waterkloof suburb with a large bundle of washing on the handlebars. It was such a cold mid-winter morning that I was shivering all over. I had on a very light, frayed and torn blazer. Nose, lips, ears, toes and fingers felt like some fat objects detached from the rest of the body, but so much part of me that the cold burnt into my nerve ends.

I came to a circle. Instead of turning to my right I didn't. I couldn't. The handlebars of the bicycle couldn't turn owing to the pressure of the bundle. From the opposite direction a handful of white boys came cycling towards me. They took their bend, but it was just when my bicycle was heading for the sidewalk of the bend. They were riding abreast. For some reason or other I did not apply my brakes. Perhaps my mind was preoccupied with the very easy yet not so very easy task of turning the handlebars. I ran into the first boy in the row, who fell on to the next, and their row was disorganized. The vehicle I was riding went to hit against the kerb, and I was down on the ground almost in a split second.

'Bastard!' shouted the boy who had fallen first.

His friends came to me and about three of them each gave me a hard kick on my backside and thighs. And they cursed and cursed and then rode away, leaving me with the cold, the pain, the numbness, and a punctured and bent front wheel.

I picked up the bundle and dragged myself on to the

side walk and leant against a tree. At first I was too
bewildered to think. I started off again and limped six
miles home. My aunt and grandmother groused and
groused before they had Oompie's vehicle fixed.

'Say it again,' said China from the lower end of Second
Avenue. I related the story of my collision again.

'You country sheep!' said Moloi, the boy next door,
laughing.

'What d'you think this is – Pietersburg forests?' was
Ratau's sarcasm.

It was a joke to all but Ratau. He was a grave-looking
boy. Little Links looked indifferent. Even when he said,
'That's the first lesson, you've got to go about town with
your eyes open.'

I had stopped worrying over being called 'skapie' –
sheep – I was told that's the label they stuck on to anybody
fresh from the country.

NOTES

Maupaneng: a village seventy-five miles outside Pietersburg
where the author spent some of his earliest years

Mealie-meal: a paste made out of maize and the staple diet of
most African families in South Africa

Fah-fee: an illegal Chinese gambling game

OTHER BOOKS BY EZEKIEL MPHAHLELE

Man must live and other stories (African Bookman, 1947)

The living and dead and other stories (Ibadan University Press,
1961)

The African Image (Faber & Faber, 1962)

ABIOSEH NICOL

ABIOSEH NICOL is from Sierra Leone. He was educated in Nigeria, Sierra Leone and at Universities in Britain. His poems and short stories have been broadcast by the B.B.C. and have appeared in a number of English and American magazines and newspapers.

As the Night the Day is set in a school in West Africa and is an interesting story of the relationship and attitudes of boys towards one another and towards their masters. The ending shows the veiled prejudice and discrimination still present even in modern West Africa, where 'you cannot hope for too much from a Syrian boy'.

As the Night the Day

Kojo and Bandele walked slowly across the hot green lawn, holding their science manuals with moist fingers. In the distance they could hear the junior school collecting in the hall of the main school building, for singing practice. Nearer, but still far enough, their classmates were strolling towards them. The two reached the science block and entered it. It was a low building set apart from the rest of the high school which sprawled on the hillside of the African savanna. The laboratory was a longish room and at one end they saw Basu, another boy, looking out of the window, his back turned to them. Mr Abu, the room and at one end they saw Basu, another boy, looking out of the window, his back turned to them. Mr Abu, the ferocious laboratory attendant, was not about. The rows of multicoloured bottles looked inviting. A bunsen burner soughed loudly in the heavy weary heat. Where the tip of the light-blue triangle of flame ended, a shimmering plastic transparency started. One could see the restless hot air moving in the minute tornado. The two African boys watched it, interestedly, holding hands.

'They say it is hotter inside the flame than on its surface,' Kojo said, doubtfully. 'I wonder how they know.'

'I think you mean the opposite; let's try it ourselves,' Bandele answered.

'How?'

'Let's take the temperature inside.'

'All right, here is a thermometer. You do it.'

'It says ninety degrees now. I shall take the temperature of the outer flame first, then you can take the inner yellow one.'

Bandele held the thermometer gently forward to the flame and Kojo craned to see. The thin thread of quick-silver shot upward within the stem of the instrument with swift malevolence and there was a slight crack. The stem had broken. On the bench the small bulbous drops of mercury which had spilled from it shivered with glinting, playful malice and shuddered down to the cement floor, dashing themselves into a thousand shining pieces, some of which coalesced again and shook gaily as if with silent laughter.

'Oh my God!' whispered Kojo hoarsely.

'Shut up!' Bandele said, imperiously, in a low voice.

Bandele swept the few drops on the bench into his cupped hand and threw the blob of mercury down the sink. He swept those on the floor under an adjoining cupboard with his bare feet. Then, picking up the broken halves of the thermometer, he tiptoed to the waste bin and

'Oh my God!' whispered Kojo hoarsely

dropped them in. He tiptoed back to Kojo, who was standing petrified by the blackboard.

'See no evil, hear no evil, speak no evil,' he whispered to Kojo.

It all took place in a few seconds. Then the rest of the class started pouring in, chattering and pushing each other. Basu, who had been at the end of the room with his back turned to them all the time, now turned round and limped laboriously across to join the class, his eyes screwed up as they always were.

The class ranged itself loosely in a semi-circle around the demonstration platform. They were dressed in the school uniform of white shirt and khaki shorts. Their official age was around sixteen although, in fact, it ranged from Kojo's fifteen years to one or two boys of twenty-one.

Mr Abu, the laboratory attendant, came in from the adjoining store and briskly cleaned the blackboard. He was a retired African sergeant from the Army Medical Corps and was feared by the boys. If he caught any of them in any petty thieving, he offered them the choice of a hard smack on the bottom or of being reported to the science masters. Most boys chose the former as they knew the matter would end there with no protracted interviews, moral recrimination, and an entry in the conduct book.

The science master stepped in and stood on his small platform. A tall, thin, dignified Negro, with greying hair and silver-rimmed spectacles badly fitting on his broad nose and always slipping down, making him look avuncular. 'Vernier' was his nickname as he insisted on exact measurement and exact speech 'as fine as a vernier scale', he would say, which measured, of course, things in thousandths of a millimetre. Vernier set the experiments for the day and demonstrated them, then retired behind the *Church Times* which he read seriously in between walking quickly down the aisles of lab. benches, advising boys. It was a simple heat experiment to show that a dark surface gave out more heat by radiation than a bright surface.

During the class, Vernier was called away to the telephone and Abu was not about, having retired to the lavatory for a smoke. As soon as a posted sentinel announced that he was out of sight, minor pandemonium broke out. Some of the boys raided the store. The wealthier ones swiped rubber tubing to make catapults and to repair bicycles, and helped themselves to chemicals for developing photographic films. The poorer boys were in deadlier earnest and took only things of strict commercial interest which could be sold easily in the market. They emptied stuff into bottles in their pockets. Soda for making soap, magnesium sulphate for opening medicine, salt for cooking, liquid paraffin for women's hairdressing, and fine yellow iodoform powder much in demand for sprinkling on sores. Kojo protested mildly against all this. 'Oh, shut up!' a few boys said. Sorie, a huge boy who always wore a fez indoors and who, rumour said, had already fathered a child, commanded respect and some leadership in the class. He was sipping his favourite mixture of diluted alcohol and bicarbonate – which he called 'gin and fizz' – from a beaker. 'Look here, Kojo, you are getting out of hand. What do you think our parents pay taxes and school fees for? For us to enjoy – or to buy a new car every year for Simpson?' The other boys laughed. Simpson was the European headmaster, feared by the small boys, adored by the boys in the middle school, and liked, in a critical fashion, with reservations, by some of the senior boys and African masters. He had a passion for new motor-cars, buying one yearly.

'Come to think of it,' Sorie continued to Kojo, 'you must take something yourself, then we'll know we are safe.' 'Yes, you must,' the other boys insisted. Kojo gave in and, unwillingly, took a little nitrate for some gunpowder experiments which he was carrying out at home.

'Someone!' the look-out called.

The boys dispersed in a moment. Sorie swilled out his mouth at the sink with some water. Mr Abu, the lab. attendant, entered and observed the innocent collective expression of the class. He glared round suspiciously and sniffed the air. It was a physics experiment, but the place smelled chemical. However, Vernier came in then. After asking if anyone was in difficulties, and finding that no one could momentarily think up anything, he retired to his chair and settled down to an article on Christian reunion, adjusting his spectacles and thoughtfully sucking an empty tooth-socket.

Towards the end of the period, the class collected around Vernier and gave in their results, which were then discussed. One of the more political boys asked Vernier: if dark surfaces gave out more heat, was that why they all had black faces in West Africa? A few boys giggled. Basu looked down and tapped his clubfoot embarrassedly on the floor. Vernier was used to questions of this sort from the senior boys. He never committed himself as he was getting near retirement and his pension, and became more guarded each year. He sometimes even feared that Simpson had spies among the boys.

'That may be so, although the opposite might be more convenient.'

Everything in science had a loophole, the boys thought, and said so to Vernier.

'Ah! that is what is called research,' he replied, enigmatically.

Sorie asked a question. Last time, they had been shown that an electric spark with hydrogen and oxygen atoms formed water. Why was not that method used to provide water in town at the height of the dry season when there was an acute water shortage?

'It would be too expensive,' Vernier replied, shortly. He disliked Sorie, not because of his different religion, but because he thought that Sorie was a bad influence and also asked ridiculous questions.

Sorie persisted. There was plenty of water during the rainy season. It could be split by lightning to hydrogen and oxygen in October and the gases compressed and stored, then changed back to water in March during the shortage. There was a faint ripple of applause from Sorie's admirers.

'It is an impracticable idea,' Vernier snapped.

The class dispersed and started walking back across the hot grass. Kojo and Bandele heaved sighs of relief and joined Sorie's crowd which was always the largest.

'Science is a bit of a swindle,' Sorie was saying. 'I do not for a moment think that Vernier believes any of it himself,' he continued. 'Because, if he does, why is he always reading religious books?'

'Come back, all of you, come back!' Mr Abu's stentorian voice rang out, across to them.

They wavered and stopped. Kojo kept walking on in a blind panic.

'Stop,' Bandele hissed across. 'You fool.' He stopped, turned and joined the returning crowd, closely followed by Bandele. Abu joined Vernier on the platform. The loose semicircle of boys faced them.

'Mr Abu just found this in the waste bin,' Vernier announced, grey with anger. He held up the two broken halves of the thermometer. 'It must be due to someone from this class as the number of thermometers was checked before being put out.'

A little wind gusted in through the window and blew the silence heavily this way and that.

'Who?'

No one answered. Vernier looked round and waited.

'Since no one has owned up, I am afraid I shall have to detain you for an hour after school as punishment,' said Vernier.

There was a murmur of dismay and anger. An important soccer house-match was scheduled for that afternoon. Some boys put their hands up and said that they had to play in the match.

'I don't care,' Vernier shouted. He felt, in any case, that too much time was devoted to games and not enough to work.

He left Mr Abu in charge and went off to fetch his things from the main building.

'We shall play "Bible and Key",' Abu announced as soon as Vernier had left. Kojo had been afraid of this and new beads of perspiration sprang from his troubled brow. All the boys knew the details. It was a method of finding out a culprit by divination. A large doorkey was placed between the leaves of a Bible at the New Testament passage where Ananias and Sapphira were struck dead before the Apostles for lying, and the Bible suspended by two bits of string tied to both ends of the key. The combination was held up by someone and the names of all present were called out in turn. When that of the sinner was called, the Bible was expected to turn round and round violently and fall.

Now Abu asked for a Bible. Someone produced a copy. He opened the first page and then shook his head and handed it back. 'This won't do,' he said, 'it's a Revised Version; only the genuine Word of God will give us the answer.'

An Authorized King James Version was then produced and he was satisfied. Soon he had the contraption fixed up. He looked round the semi-circle from Sorie at one end, through the others, to Bandele, Basu, and Kojo at the other, near the door.

'You seem to have an honest face,' he said to Kojo. 'Come and hold it.' Kojo took the ends of the string gingerly with both hands, trembling slightly.

Abu moved over to the low window and stood at

attention, his sharp profile outlined against the red
hibiscus flowers, the green trees, and the molten sky. The
boys watched anxiously. A black-bodied lizard scurried
up a wall and started nodding its pink head with grave
impartiality.

Abu fixed his ageing bloodshot eyes on the suspended
Bible. He spoke hoarsely and slowly:

> 'Oh, Bible, Bible, on a key,
> Kindly tell it unto me,
> By swinging slowly round and true,
> To whom this sinful act is due. . . .'

He turned to the boys and barked out their names in a
parade-ground voice, beginning with Sorie and working
his way round, looking at the Bible after each name.

To Kojo, trembling and shivering as if ice-cold water
had been thrown over him, it seemed as if he had lost
all power and that some gigantic being stood behind him
holding up his tired aching elbows. It seemed to him as
if the key and Bible had taken on a life of their own, and
he watched with fascination the whole combination
moving slowly, jerkily, and rhythmically in short arcs as
if it had acquired a heart-beat.

'Ayo Sogbenri, Sonnir Kargbo, Oji Ndebu.' Abu was
coming to the end now. 'Tommy Longe, Ajayi Cole,
Bandele Fagb . . .'

Kojo dropped the Bible. 'I am tired,' he said, in a small
scream. 'I am tired.'

'Yes, he is,' Abu agreed, 'but we are almost finished;
only Bandele and Basu are left.'

'Pick up that book, Kojo, and hold it up again.' Bandele's voice whipped through the air with cold fury. It
sobered Kojo and he picked it up.

'Will you continue please with my name, Mr Abu?'
Bandele asked, turning to the window.

'Go back to your place quickly, Kojo,' Abu said.

'Vernier is coming. He might be vexed. He is a strongly religious man and so does not believe in the Bible-and-key ceremony.'

Kojo slipped back with sick relief, just before Vernier entered.

In the distance the rest of the school were assembling for closing prayers. The class sat and stood around the blackboard and demonstration bench in attitudes of exasperation, resignation, and self-righteous indignation. Kojo's heart was beating so loudly that he was surprised no one else heard it.

> 'Once to every man and nation
> Comes the moment to decide . . .'

The closing hymn floated across to them, interrupting the still afternoon.

Kojo got up. He felt now that he must speak the truth, or life would be intolerable ever afterwards. Bandele got up swiftly before him. In fact, several things seemed to happen all at the same time. The rest of the class stirred. Vernier looked up from a book review which he had started reading. A butterfly, with black and gold wings, flew in and sat on the edge of the blackboard, flapping its wings quietly and waiting too.

'Basu was here first before any of the class,' Bandele said firmly.

Everyone turned to Basu, who cleared his throat.

'I was just going to say so myself, sir,' Basu replied to Vernier's inquiring glance.

'Pity you had no thought of it before,' Vernier said, dryly. 'What were you doing here?'

'I missed the previous class, so I came straight to the lab. and waited. I was over there by the window, trying to look at the blue sky. I did not break the thermometer, sir.'

A few boys tittered. Some looked away. The others muttered. Basu's breath always smelt of onions, but although he could play no games, some boys liked him and were kind to him in a tolerant way.

'Well if you did not, someone did. We shall continue with the detention.'

Vernier noticed Abu standing by. 'You need not stay, Mr Abu,' he said to him. 'I shall close up. In fact, come with me now and I shall let you out through the back gate.'

He went out with Abu.

When he had left, Sorie turned to Basu and asked mildly:

'You are sure you did not break it?'

'No, I didn't.'

'He did it,' someone shouted.

'But what about the Bible-and-key?' Basu protested. 'It did not finish. Look at him.' He pointed to Bandele.

'I was quite willing for it to go on,' said Bandele. 'You were the only one left.'

Someone threw a book at Basu and said, 'Confess!'

Basu backed on to a wall. 'To God, I shall call the police if anyone strikes me,' he cried fiercely.

'He thinks he can buy the police,' a voice called.

'That proves it,' someone shouted from the back.

'Yes, he must have done it,' the others said, and they started throwing books at Basu. Sorie waved his arm for them to stop, but they did not. Books, corks, boxes of matches rained on Basu. He bent his head and shielded his face with his bent arm.

'I did not do it, I swear I did not do it. Stop it, you fellows,' he moaned over and over again. A small cut had appeared on his temple and he was bleeding. Kojo sat quietly for a while. Then a curious hum started to pass through him, and his hands began to tremble, his armpits to feel curiously wetter. He turned round and picked up a book and flung it with desperate force at Basu, and then another. He felt somehow that there was an awful swelling of guilt which he could only shed by punishing himself through hurting someone. Anger and rage against everything different seized him, because if everything and everyone had been the same, somehow he felt nothing would have been wrong and they would all have been happy. He was carried away now by a torrent which swirled and pounded. He felt that somehow Basu was in the wrong, must be in the wrong, and if he hurt him hard enough he would convince the others and therefore himself that he had not broken the thermometer and that he had never done anything wrong. He groped for something bulky enough to throw, and picked up the Bible.

'Stop it,' Vernier shouted through the open doorway. 'Stop it, you hooligans, you beasts.'

They all became quiet and shamefacedly put down what they were going to throw. Basu was crying quietly and hopelessly, his thin body shaking.

'Go home, all of you, go home. I am ashamed of you.' His black face shone with anger. 'You are an utter disgrace to your nation and to your race.'

They crept away, quietly, uneasily, avoiding each other's eyes, like people caught in a secret passion.

Vernier went to the first-aid cupboard and started dressing Basu's wounds.

Kojo and Bandele came back and hid behind the door, listening. Bandele insisted that they should.

Vernier put Basu's bandaged head against his waistcoat and dried the boy's tears with his handkerchief, gently patting his shaking shoulders.

'It wouldn't have been so bad if I had done it, sir,' he mumbled, snuggling his head against Vernier, 'but I did not do it. I swear to God I did not.'

'Hush, hush,' said Vernier comfortingly.

'Now they will hate me even more,' he moaned.

'Hush, hush.'

'I don't mind the wounds so much, they will heal.'

'Hush, hush.'

'They've missed the football match and now they will never talk to me again, oh-ee, oh-ee, why have I been so punished?'

'As you grow older,' Vernier advised, 'you must learn that men are punished not always for what they do, but often for what people think they will do, or for what they are. Remember that and you will find it easier to forgive them. "To thine own self be true!"' Vernier ended with a flourish, holding up his clenched fist in a mock dramatic gesture, quoting from the Shakespeare examination set-book for the year and declaiming to the dripping taps and empty benches and still afternoon, to make Basu laugh.

Basu dried his eyes and smiled wanly and replied: '"And it shall follow as the night the day." Hamlet, Act One, Scene Three, Polonius to Laertes.'

'There's a good chap. First Class Grade One. I shall give you a lift home.'

Kojo and Bandele walked down the red laterite road together, Kojo dispiritedly kicking stones into the gutter.

'The fuss they made over a silly old thermometer,' Bandele began.

'I don't know, old man, I don't know,' Kojo said impatiently.

They had both been shaken by the scene in the empty lab. A thin invisible wall of hostility and mistrust was slowly rising between them.

'Basu did not do it, of course,' Bandele said.

Kojo stopped dead in his tracks. 'Of course he did not do it,' he shouted; 'we did it.'

'No need to shout, old man. After all, it was your idea.'

'It wasn't,' Kojo said furiously. 'You suggested we try it.'

'Well, you started the argument. Don't be childish.'

They tramped on silently, raising small clouds of dust with their bare feet.

'I should not take it too much to heart,' Bandele continued. 'That chap Basu's father hoards foodstuff like rice and palm oil until there is a shortage and then sells them at high prices. The police are watching him.'

'What has that got to do with it?' Kojo asked.

'Don't you see, Basu might quite easily have broken that thermometer. I bet he has done things before that we have all been punished for.' Bandele was emphatic.

They walked on steadily down the main road of the town, past the Syrian and Lebanese shops crammed with knick-knacks and rolls of cloth, past a large Indian shop with dull red carpets and brass trays displayed in its windows, carefully stepping aside in the narrow road as the British officials sped by in cars to their hill-station bungalows for lunch and siesta.

Kojo reached home at last. He washed his feet and ate his main meal for the day. He sat about heavily and restlessly for some hours. Night soon fell with its usual swiftness, at six, and he finished his homework early and went to bed.

Lying in bed he rehearsed again what he was determined to do the next day. He would go up to Vernier:

'Sir,' he would begin, 'I wish to speak with you privately.'

'Can it wait?' Vernier would ask.

'No, sir,' he would say firmly, 'as a matter of fact it is rather urgent.'

Vernier would take him to an empty classroom and say, 'What is troubling you, Kojo Anànse?'

'I wish to make a confession, sir. I broke the thermometer yesterday.' He had decided he would not name Bandele; it was up to the latter to decide whether he would lead a pure life.

C

Vernier would adjust his slipping glasses up his nose and think. Then he would say:

'This is a serious matter, Kojo. You realize you should have confessed yesterday?'

'Yes, sir, I am very sorry.'

'You have done great harm, but better late than never. You will, of course, apologize in front of the class and particularly to Basu who has shown himself a finer chap than all of you.'

'I shall do so, sir.'

'Why have you come to me now to apologize? Were you hoping that I would simply forgive you?'

'I was hoping you would, sir. I was hoping you would show your forgiveness by beating me.'

Vernier would pull his glasses up his nose again. He would move his tongue inside his mouth reflectively. 'I think you are right. Do you feel you deserve six strokes or nine?'

'Nine, sir.'

'Bend over!'

Kojo had decided he would not cry because he was almost a man.

Whack! Whack!!

Lying in bed in the dark thinking about it all as it would happen tomorrow, he clenched his teeth and tensed his buttocks in imaginary pain.

Whack! Whack!! Whack!!!

Suddenly, in his little room, under his thin cotton sheet, he began to cry. Because he felt the sharp lancing pain already cutting into him. Because of Basu and Simpson and the thermometer. For all the things he wanted to do and be which would never happen. For all the good men they had told them about, Jesus Christ, Mohammed, and George Washington who never told a lie. For Florence Nightingale and David Livingstone. For

Kagawa, the Japanese man, for Gandhi, and for Kwegyir Aggrey, the African. Oh-ee, oh-ee. Because he knew he would never be as straight and strong and true as the school song said they should be. He saw, for the first time, what this thing would be like, becoming a man. He touched the edge of an inconsolable eternal grief. Oh-ee, oh-ee; always, he felt, always I shall be a disgrace to the nation and the race.

His mother passed by his bedroom door, slowly dragging her slippered feet as she always did. He pushed his face into his wet pillow to stifle his sobs, but she had heard him. She came in and switched on the light.

'What is the matter with you, my son?'

He pushed his face farther into his pillow.

'Nothing,' he said, muffled and choking.

'You have been looking like a sick fowl all afternoon,' she continued.

She advanced and put the back of her moist cool fingers against the side of his neck.

'You have got fever,' she exclaimed. 'I'll get something from the kitchen.'

When she had gone out, Kojo dried his tears and turned the dry side of the pillow up. His mother reappeared with a thermometer in one hand and some quinine mixture in the other.

'Oh, take it away, take it away,' he shouted, pointing to her right hand and shutting his eyes tightly.

'All right, all right,' she said, slipping the thermometer into her bosom.

He is a queer boy, she thought, with pride and a little fear as she watched him drink the clear bitter fluid.

She then stood by him and held his head against her broad thigh as he sat up on the low bed, and she stroked his face. She knew he had been crying but did not ask him why, because she was sure he would not tell her. She knew he was learning, first slowly and now quickly,

and she would soon cease to be his mother and be only
one of the womenfolk in the family. Such a short time,
she thought, when they are really yours and tell you
everything. She sighed and slowly eased his sleeping head
down gently.

The next day Kojo got to school early, and set to things
briskly. He told Bandele that he was going to confess but
would not name him. He half hoped he would join him.
But Bandele had said, threateningly, that he had better
not mention his name, let him go and be a Boy Scout
on his own. The sneer strengthened him and he went
off to the lab. He met Mr Abu and asked for Vernier.
Abu said Vernier was busy and what was the matter,
anyhow.

'I broke the thermometer yesterday,' Kojo said in a
businesslike manner.

Abu put down the glassware he was carrying.

'Well, I never!' he said. 'What do you think you will
gain by this?'

'I broke it,' Kojo repeated.

'Basu broke it,' Abu said impatiently. 'Sorie got him
to confess and Basu himself came here this morning and
told the science master and myself that he knew now
that he had knocked the thermometer by mistake when
he came in early yesterday afternoon. He had not turned
round to look, but he had definitely heard a tinkle as
he walked by. Someone must have picked it up and put
it in the waste bin. The whole matter is settled, the
palaver finished.'

He tapped a barometer on the wall and, squinting,
read the pressure. He turned again to Kojo.

'I should normally have expected him to say so yesterday and save you boys missing the game. But there you
are,' he added, shrugging and trying to look reasonable,
'you cannot hope for too much from a Syrian boy.'

RICHARD RIVE

RICHARD RIVE was born in Cape Town, South Africa, in 1931. After winning a municipal scholarship, he went on to High School and afterwards graduated in English from the University of Cape Town. He qualified as a teacher at Hewat Training College. His stories first appeared in South African periodicals and after they had won the attention of critics were published in many languages. *African Songs*, his collection of short stories, appeared in 1963. In the preceding year he was awarded a Farfield Foundation Fellowship and travelled widely in Africa and Europe. His first novel, *Emergency*, is about to be published.

Resurrection is set against the discrimination practised within the mixed community in South Africa. Here the fairer will shun the darker-skinned because of the possibility of crossing the line. The dark mother is dead, and her white children and one dark daughter are sitting round her coffin waiting for the priest to perform the last rites.

Resurrection

And still the people sang. And one by one, the voices joined in and the volume rose. Tremulously at first, thin and tenuous, and then swelling till it filled the tiny dining-room, pulsated into the two bedrooms, stacked high with hats and overcoats, and spent itself in the kitchen where fussy housewives, dressed in black, were making wreaths.

> Jesu, lover of my soul,
> Let me to Thy Bo-som fly . . .

A blubbery woman in the corner nearest the cheap, highly-polished chest of drawers wept hysterically. Above her head hung a cheap reproduction of a Karroo scene. A dazzling white-gabled farmhouse baking in the hot African sun. In the distance *koppies* shimmered against a hazy blue sky. Her bosom heaved convulsively as she refused to be placated. Her tears proved infectious and her lips quivered and handkerchiefs were convulsively sought.

> Hide me, O my Saviour hide,
> Till the storm of life is past,
> Safe into the haven guide . . .

sang a small boy in a freshly laundered Eton collar who shared a stiff Ancient and Modern hymn-book with his mother. His voice was wiry and weak and completely dominated by the strong soprano next to him. All the people joined in and sang. Except Mavis. Only Mavis sat silent, glossy-eyed, staring down at her rough, though delicately shaped brown hands. Her eyes, hot and red, but tearless, with a slightly contemptuous sneer around the closed, cruel mouth. Only Mavis sat silent. Staring at her hands and noticing that the left thumbnail was scarred and broken. She refused to raise her eyes, refused to look at the coffin, at the hymn-book open and neglected in her lap. Her mouth was tightly shut, as if determined not to open, not to say a word. Tensely she sat and stared at her broken thumbnail. The room did not exist. The fat woman blubbered unnoticed. The people sang but Mavis heard nothing.

Only Mavis sat silent

Other refuge have I none,
Hangs my helpless soul on Thee . . .

they began the second verse. The fat woman had sufficiently recovered to attempt to add a tremulous contralto. The boy in the Eton collar laboriously followed the line with his finger. Mavis vaguely recognized Rosie as she fussily hurried in with a tray of fresh flowers, passed a brief word with an overdressed woman nearest the door, and busily hurried out again. Mavis sensed things happening but saw without seeing and felt without feeling. Nothing registered, but she could feel the Old-Woman's presence, could feel the room becoming her dead mother, becoming full of Ma, crowded with Ma, swirling with Ma. Ma of the gnarled hands and frightened eyes.

Those eyes that had asked questioningly, 'Mavis, why do they treat me so? Please, Mavis, why do they treat me so?'

And Mavis had known the answer and had felt the anger well up inside her, till her mouth felt hot and raw. And she had spat out at the Old-Woman, 'Because you're coloured! You're coloured, Ma, but you gave birth to white children. It's your fault, Ma, all your fault. . . . You gave birth to white children. White children, Ma, white children!'

Mavis felt dimly aware that the room was overcrowded, overbearingly overcrowded, hot, stuffy, crammed, over-flowing. And of course, Ma. Squeezed in. Occupying a tiny place in the centre. Right in the centre. Pride of place in a coffin of pinewood which bore the economical legend,

Maria Loupser
1889–1961
R.I.P.

Rest in Peace. With people crowding around and sharing seats and filling the doorway. And Ma had been that

Maria Loupser who must now rest in peace. Maria
Loupser. Maria Wilhemina Loupser. Mavis looked up
quickly, to see if the plaque was really there, then auto-
matically shifted her gaze to her broken nail. No one
noticed her self-absorption, and the singing continued un-
interruptedly:

> Other refuge have I none,
> Hangs my helpless soul on Thee . . .

Flowers. Hot, oppressive smell of flowers. Flowers, death
and the people singing. A florid, red-faced man in the
doorway singing so that his veins stood out purple against
the temples. People bustling in and out. Fussily. Coming
to have a look at Ma. A last look at Ma. To put a flower
in the coffin for Ma. Then opening hymn-books and singing a dirge for Ma. Poor deceived Ma of the tragic eyes
and twisted hands who had given birth to White children,
and Mavis. Now they raised their voices and sang for
Ma.

> Leave, ah leave me not alone,
> Still support and comfort me . . .

And it had been only a month earlier when Mavis had
looked into those bewildered eyes.
'Mavis, why do they treat me so?'
And Mavis had become angry so that her saliva had
turned hot in her mouth.
'Please, Mavis, why do they treat me so?'
And then she had driven the words into the Old-Woman
with a skewer.
'Because you are old and black, and your children want
you out of the way.'
And yet what Mavis wanted to add was:
'They want me out of the way too, Ma, because you
made me black like you. I am also your child, Ma. I
belong to you. They want me also to stay in the kitchen

and use the back door. We must not be seen, Ma, their friends must not see us. We embarrass them, Ma, so they hate us. They hate us because we're black. You and me, Ma.'

But she had not said so, and had only stared cruelly into the eyes of the Old-Woman.

'You're no longer useful, Ma. You're a nuisance, a bloody nuisance, a bloody black nuisance. You might come out of your kitchen and shock the white scum they bring here. You're a bloody nuisance, Ma!'

But still the Old-Woman could not understand, and looked helplessly at Mavis.

'But I don't want to go in the dining-room. It's true, Mavis, I don't want to go in the dining-room.' And as she spoke the tears flooded her eyes and she whimpered like a child who had lost a toy. 'It's my dining-room, Mavis, it's true. It's my dining-room.'

And Mavis had felt a dark and hideous pleasure over-whelming her so that she screamed hysterically at the Old-Woman, 'You're black and your bloody children's white. Jim and Rosie and Sonny are white, white, white! And you made me. You made me black!'

Then Mavis had broken down exhausted at her self-revealing and had cried like a baby.

'Ma, why did you make me black?'

And then only had a vague understanding strayed into those milky eyes, and Ma had taken her youngest into her arms and rocked and soothed her. And crooned to her in a cracked, broken voice the songs she had sung years before she had come to Cape Town.

> Slaap, my kindjie, slaap sag,
> Onder engele vannag . . .

And the voice of the Old-Woman had become stronger and more perceptive as her dull eyes saw her childhood, and the stream running through Wolfgat, and the broken-

down church, and the moon rising in the direction of
Solitaire.

And Ma had understood and rocked Mavis in her arms
like years before. And now Ma was back in the dining-
room as shadows crept across the wall.

Abide with me, fast falls the eventide . . .

Shadows creeping across the room. Shadows grey and
deep. As deep as Ma's ignorance.

The darkness deepens; Lord, with me abide . . .

Shadows filtering through the drawn blind. Rosie
tight-lipped and officious. Sonny. Jim who had left his
white wife at home. Pointedly ignoring Mavis: speaking
in hushed tones to the florid man in the doorway. Mavis,
a small inconspicuous brown figure in the corner. The
only other brown face in the crowded dining-room besides
Ma. Even the Old-Woman was paler in death. Ma's
friends in the kitchen. A huddled, frightened group
around the stove.

'Mavis, why do they tell my friends not to visit me?'

And Mavis had shrugged her shoulders indifferently.

'Please, Mavis, why do they tell my friends not to visit
me?'

And Mavis has turned on her. 'Do you want Soufie
with her black skin to sit in the dining-room? Or Ou Kaar
with his *kroeskop*? Or Eva or Leuntjie? Do you? Do you
want Sonny's wife to see them? Or the white dirt Rosie
picks up? Do you want to shame your children? Humiliate
them? Expose their black blood?'

And the Old-Woman had blubbered, 'I only want my
friends to visit me. They can sit in the kitchen.'

And Mavis had sighed helplessly at the simplicity of the
doddering Old-Woman and had felt like saying, 'And

what of my friends, my coloured friends? Must they also sit in the kitchen?'

And tears had shot into those milky eyes and the mother had looked even older. 'Mavis, I want my friends to visit me, even if they sit in the kitchen. Please, Mavis, they're all I got.'

And now Ma's friends sat in the kitchen, a cowed timid group round the fire, speaking the raw guttural Afrikaans of the Caledon District. They spoke of Ma and their childhood together. Ou Kaar and Leuntjie and Eva and Ma. Of the Caledon District, cut off from bustling Cape Town. Where the Moravian Mission Church was crumbling, and the sweet water ran past Wolfgat, and past Karwyderskraal, and lost itself near Grootkop. And the moon rose rich and yellow from the hills behind Solitaire. And now they sat frightened and huddled around the stove, speaking of Ma. Tant Soufie in a new *kopdoek*, and Ou Kaar conspicuous in borrowed yellow shoes, sizes too small. And Leuntjie and Eva.

And in the dining-room sat Dadda's relations, singing. Dadda's friends who had ignored Ma while she had lived. Dadda's white friends and relations, and a glossy-eyed Mavis, a Mavis who scratched meaninglessly at her broken thumbnail. And now the singing rose in volume as still more people filed in.

> When other helpers fail and comforts flee,
> Help of the helpless, O abide with me. . . .

they sang to the dead woman.

Mavis could have helped Ma, could have given the understanding she needed, could have protected Ma, have tried to stop the petty tyranny. But she had never tried to reason with them. Rosie, Sonny and Jim. She had never pleaded with them, explained to them that the Old-Woman was dying. Her own soul ate her up. Gnawed her inside. She was afraid of their reactions should they notice her. Preferred to play a shadow, seen but never heard. A vague entity, part of the furniture. If only they could somehow be aware of her emotions. The feelings bottled up inside her, the bubbling volcano below. She was afraid they might openly say, 'Why don't you both clear out and leave us in peace, you bloody black bastards?' She could then have cleared out, should then have cleared out, sought a room in Woodstock or Salt River and forgotten her frustration. But there was Ma. There was the Old-Woman. Mavis had never spoken to them, but had vented her spleen on her helpless mother.

'You sent them to a white school. You were proud of your white brats and hated me, didn't you?'

And the mother had stared with ox-like dumbness.

'You encouraged them to bring their friends to the house, to your house, and told me to stay in the kitchen. And you had a black skin yourself. You hated me, Ma, hated me! And now they've pushed you into the kitchen. There's no one to blame but you. You're the cause of all this.'

And she had tormented the Old-Woman who could not retaliate. Who could not understand. Now she sat tortured with memories as they sang hymns for Ma.

The room assumed a sepulchral atmosphere. Shadows deepening, grey then darker. Tears, flowers, handkerchiefs, and, dominating everything, the simple bewildered eyes of Ma, bewildered even in death. So Mavis had covered them with two pennies, that others might not see.

I need Thy presence every passing hour . . .

sang Dadda's eldest brother, who sat with eyes tightly shut near the head of the coffin. He had bitterly resented Dadda's marriage to a coloured woman. Living in sin! A Loupser married to a Hottentot! He had boasted of his refusal to greet Ma socially while she lived, and he attended the funeral only because his brother's wife had died. This was the second time he had been in the dining-room. The first time was Dadda's funeral. And now this. A coloured girl, his niece he believed, sitting completely out of place and saying nothing. Annoying, most annoying.

What but Thy Grace can foil the tempter's power . . .

sang the boy in the Eton collar, whose mother had not quite recovered from the shock that Mr Loupser had had a coloured wife. All sang except Mavis, torturing herself with memories.

'I am going to die, Mavis,' those milky eyes had told her a week before, 'I think I am going to die.'

'Ask your white brats to bury you. You slaved for them.'

'They are my children but they do not treat me right.'

'Do you know why? Shall I tell you why?' And she had driven home every word with an ugly ferocity. 'Because they're ashamed of you. Afraid of you, afraid the world might know of their coloured mother.'

'But I did my best for them!'

'You did more than your best, you encouraged them, but you were ashamed of me, weren't you? So now we share a room at the back where we can't be seen. And you are going to die, and your white children will thank God that you're out of the way.'

'They are your brothers and sisters, Mavis.'

'What's that you're saying?' Mavis gasped, amazed at the hypocrisy. 'What's that? I hate them and I hate you. I hate you!'

And the Old-Woman had whispered, 'But you are my children, you are all my children. Please, Mavis, don't let me die so.'

'You will die in the back room and will be buried from the kitchen.'

'It's a sin, Mavis, it's a sin!'

But they had not buried her from the kitchen. They had removed the table from the dining-room and had borrowed chairs from the neighbours. And now while they waited for the priest from Dadda's church, they sang hymns.

> Heaven's morning breaks, and earth's vain shadows flee . . .

sang the boy in the Eton collar.

> In life, in death, O Lord, abide with me.

The florid man sang loudly to end the verse. There was an expectant bustle at the door, and then the Priest from Dadda's church, St John the Divine, appeared. All now crowded into the dining-room, those who were making wreaths, and Tant Soufie holding Ou Kaar's trembling hand.

'Please, Mavis, ask Father Josephs at the Mission to bury me.'

'Ask your brats to fetch him themselves. See them ask a black man to bury you!'

'Please, Mavis, see that Father Josephs buries me!'

'It's not my business, you fool! You did nothing for me!'

'I am your mother, my girl,' the Old-Woman had sobbed, 'I raised you.'

'Yes, you raised me, and you taught me my place! You took me to the Mission with you, because we are too black to go to St John's. Let them see Father Josephs for a change. Let them enter our Mission and see our God.'

And Ma had not understood but whimpered, 'Please, Mavis, let Father Josephs bury me.'

So now the Priest from Dadda's church stood at the head of her coffin, sharp and thin, clutching his cassock with the left hand, while his right held an open prayer-book.

> I said I will take heed to my ways:
> that I offend not in my tongue.
> I will keep my mouth as it were with
> a bridle: while the ungodly is in my sight.

Mavis felt the cruel irony of the words.

> I held my tongue and spake nothing.
> I kept silent, yea even from good words
> but it was pain and grief to me . . .

The fat lady stroked her son's head and sniffed loudly.

> My heart was hot within me, and while I
> was thus musing the fire kindled, and at
> the last I spake with my tongue . . .

Mavis now stared entranced at her broken thumbnail. The words seared and, filling, dominated the room.

It was true. Rosie had consulted her about going to the Mission and asking for Father Josephs, but she had turned on her heel without a word and walked out into the streets, and walked and walked. Through the cobbled streets of older Cape Town, up beyond the Mosque in the Malay Quarter on the slopes of Signal Hill. Thinking of the dead woman in the room.

A mother married to a white man and dying in a back room. Walking the streets, the Old-Woman with her, followed by the Old-Woman's eyes. Eating out her soul. Let them go to the Mission and see our God. Meet Father Josephs. But they had gone for Dadda's Priest who now prayed at the coffin of a broken coloured woman. And the back room was empty.

'I heard a voice from heaven, Saying unto me, Write, From henceforth blessed are the dead which die in the Lord: Even so saith the Spirit; for they rest from their labours. . . .

'Lord take Thy servant, Maria Wilhemina Loupser,

into Thy eternal care. Grant her Thy eternal peace and understanding. Thou art our refuge and our rock. Look kindly upon her children who even in this time of trial and suffering look up to Thee for solace. Send Thy eternal blessing upon them, for they have heeded Thy commandment which is Honour thy father and thy mother, that thy days may be long . . .'

Mavis felt hot, strangely, unbearably hot. Her saliva turned to white heat in her mouth and her head rolled drunkenly. The room was filled with her mother's presence, her mother's eyes, body, soul. Flowing into her, filling every pore, becoming one with her, becoming a living condemnation.

'Misbelievers!' she screeched hoarsely. 'Liars! You killed me! You murdered me! Don't you know your God?'

NOTES

koppies : low hills
kroeskop : curly-headed; tufted hair
kopdoek : head-scarf

OTHER BOOKS BY RICHARD RIVE

African Songs (short stories) (Seven Seas, 1963)
Emergency (Faber & Faber, 1964)
Quartet (anthology) (Crown, 1963; African Writers Series, 1965)

ALFRED HUTCHINSON

ALFRED HUTCHINSON was born at Hectorspruit in the Eastern Transvaal in 1924. Having attended St Peter's School he went on to Fort Hare where he gained a B.A. degree in English. After entering politics he was arrested on charges of high treason. He escaped and made his way to Ghana. From there he finally left for England where he now lives and teaches in a secondary modern school. He is married with three children.

After having faced charges of high treason in South Africa, Alfred Hutchinson and the rest of the accused were temporarily freed. There was an air of uncertainty: how long would they remain free before fresh indictments might be framed against them? They were on bail and there was every possibility that the trial might start all over again. A day or two later he was arrested for failing to carry a pass, but the magistrate ruled that the prosecution had failed to establish that he was African. As his grandfather was white he could be classified as coloured, one of mixed blood, which exempted him from carrying a pass. Hutchinson decided to jump his treason trial bail and escape to Ghana. Having been released from the pass charge he set off at once and with false papers he left Johannesburg by train for the North. His book, *Road to Ghana*, deals with his journey across Africa, after leaving Johannesburg with false papers, his crossing of the Rhodesian frontier, and then making his way through Portuguese East Africa into Nyasaland and on to Dar-es-Salaam where his hopes are dashed when he is arrested for entering the Territory without a permit. For a fortnight he is jailed but, after this, he is released and given

eight days in which to leave Tanganyika. Out of the blue
assistance arrives from England, as well as from Tanganyika
itself, and he is soon on his way by air to Ghana.

When leaving Bulawayo by train he had made friends with
the other people in his third-class carriage. Amongst them was
an old man who had been to Cape Town and was now returning to Nyasaland after fourteen years, and Mweli, a sickly
looking man in an expensive green hat who was also going back
to Nyasaland after an absence of six years. This excerpt from
Road to Ghana gives an account of their train journey from
Dondo in Portuguese East Africa to Blantyre in Nyasaland.

Journey to Blantyre

The man pointed back along the road we had come
and beyond the railway line into the depth of the trees.
That way were the waiting quarters for the Nyasaland
train. This was the Mtandizi – Rhodesia Native Labour
Supply Commission.

Mweli shook his head and glared at the old man. He
looked at the distance we had come and shook his head
over and over again. 'You never ask! Once you start
walking you never look back!'

The old man, suitcase on his head and one hand
collaring a sack, broke into a burdened shuffle and never
looked back. Mweli struggled along, his suitcase battering
his ankles with every step he took. I gave him my lighter
bag. 'Thank you, S'bali. A person could die travelling
with Kehla.'

This was Dondo – the junction for Nyasaland – and only
thirty miles from Beira. The spunk of the earth was in the
air – drawn by the astringent sun. It was stickily hot.

The waiting quarters swarmed with people and filth.
Refuse of numberless journeys lay scattered around.

Banana peels, mealie cobs, bits of bread, chewed-up bits of sugar-cane, tins of jam . . . Fowls scratched among the refuse. And children spun and chased one another in play.

We kicked aside a clearing in the jungle of dirt and dumped our things. Already the life of the stopping place was re-enacting itself. Smoke was rising from the cooking places and women went, pot in hand, to fetch water from the station. The men sat on their things or stood against the uprights of the shed. They talked and munched bread smeared thick with jam, waving away the flies which flourished in the cesspools of the lavatories.

Women came to the waiting quarters to trade. They had tickey bundles of wood; tickey cups of mealie meal. They sold hunks of porridge, fried catfish and sweet potatoes. The man in the guard's cap came up to me and asked me for a cigarette, and I laughed and laughed, remembering how he had got us hopelessly lost in Salisbury. He laughed too, showing gaps in his front teeth.

Then the old man was seized by a terrible meat-hunger. Every inch of his body cried for meat. He whimpered at the thought of meat and soon we were all in the throes of meat-hunger and singing: 'Nyama! Nyama! Nyama! Meat! Meat! Meat!' The old man chuckled at the idea of meat, the pleasure of meat.

And so the old man and I set out in quest of meat, leaving Mweli to cook the porridge. We passed a clinic, a hotel, two stores, a garage to which was attached a very small escola. Inside there were sounds of learning and probably an asimilado or two in the making.

'Let's go nicely, S'bali,' said the old man. 'The Portuguese are no people. They're always looking for trouble.'

We were looking for the butcher, we told people. And they pointed us up the road. The old man suddenly remembered that he wanted to buy a line and hooks for his son. We wandered into a shop where bright-eyed mulattos cheated the old man as if he were a huge joke.

Then we stumbled on meat. In a yard an antelope was being hacked up. We bought a mountain of it for four shillings and the old man's joy was complete. The anticipation of meat burned so deeply into the old man that he wanted a short cut back to the quarters. But we ran into a barbed-wire fence and the old man stopped, dismayed. He would not go through and shouted to some men near by for permission to do so.

'You don't know the Portuguese, S'bali. Just for going through that fence you could be fined ten pounds.'

The Nyasaland train has arrived. People pour into the quarters. Five hundred of us are going to Nyasaland and five hundred are going in the opposite direction. They come with their bundles on their heads, with the burdened shuffle. The voices rise into a roaring sea. Their bundles are a little more drab than ours, but even that distinction is fine. They too begin to enact the life of the stopping places; starting at the beginning.

But the whoop of Mafeking does not rise: the welcome and the rejection: the triumph jellying into unutterable agony. The abuse, the butting and cuffing, the sting of a blow where a hug would have been more appropriate ... all this is missing.

Five hundred of us are returning to Nyasaland. Five hundred have left Nyasaland. And the new-comers sit on their things or stand with the uncertainties of the road mirrored in their eyes. A sound like a hymn rises in a trough of the hubbub, only to die in neglect.

The symbol of the road appears. Men and women rise, lift their things on to their heads and shoulders and form the Indian file. First the men of Mzilikazi – the stalwarts from the mines; the men who have served their time. And it seems natural that they should rise first: that priority should be theirs. They swagger a bit, conscious of their status. The Indian file begins to move and then stops. The first steps of the burdened shuffle, and before

the full swing, another stop. And for the first time the
symbol collapses. The file breaks up in disorder and there
is a mad scramble for the coaches of the Nyasaland train.

We managed to pile into an antiquated, green, and
battered carriage. The wood was splintering and most of
the windows had lost their wooden shutters. The latch
of the door was broken and it would not stay shut.
Benches ran along the side of the carriage while a double
bench supporting a rack ran in the middle. The drinking
water was in the lavatory.

'Nyasaland! Nyasaland!' The old man stamped the
floor, emitting squeals of delight. 'You'll see, S'bali. It's
driven by a black man . . .'

'This is your train of Nyasaland,' said Mweli, wrinkling
his face with distaste. 'The Orlando trains are better, a
thousand times better . . .'

The engine let out a long huge defiant bellow ending
in a flourish. But that engine was to prove before long to
be the greatest disappointment of the whole journey. We
soon discovered that the bellow was the only thing it
had as it puffed and panted, crawling at a snail's pace.

'Noise, S'bali, nothing but noise! Slow-coach-goods-
train.' Mweli swiped the old man a venomous look.

The forest came to stand a few yards from the railway
and now the engine bellowed like a frightened ox. The
carriage lashed about like a hurt puff-adder over sand.

'I'm going to see my boy, S'bali,' said the old man.
'He's going to teach the fish a lesson with the hooks and
line I've bought him . . .'

'Big fish?'

'Bigger than you, S'bali. . . .'

'Do they know you're coming?' I asked.

'I wrote and told them, S'bali . . . I wrote. He must be
a big man now, S'bali . . . So big. . . .' The old man
indicated the height of the boy he had left fourteen
years ago.

'And your wife has waited all these years?'

'That's nothing,' said Mweli. 'Some of us go away for so long that the people begin to take us for dead. But the women wait. The laws of Nyasaland are heavy on a woman, S'bali. The women of Nyasaland are not like the women of Goli where you turn a street and they already have another husband.'

'And the men of Nyasaland?'

'A man is a dog, S'bali. A man is allowed to steal. But it's different with a woman.'

'I've left my Nkazane [girl-friend] at Cape Town,' boasted the old man, and he broke into Xhosa to exclaim again, 'Tshini, mfondini.'

Mweli was remembering the women of Johannesburg, remembering the woman with his three children that he had deserted,

'Hai, S'bali, the babies of Goli! Once they get a Nyasa they think they've found the greatest fool. They finish us Nyasas.' Mweli shook his head and laughed. 'I left her with the furniture and all. She tried to stop me by taking my pass, but I told her to keep it if she wanted to. I was going home.'

An African in a dirty shirt and green tabs cried 'Tickets' and passed on. A European followed and we held our tickets for him to clip.

'As lazy as a Bunu [South African white],' said Mweli.

Night comes. The forest takes a step towards the railway line and stands with folded arms. The engine bellows with terror. And the moon peers at us through the branches of the trees.

We sit quietly as we rock and sway as if mulling over things. The old man sits with the milk of age in his eyes while Mweli has folded himself on the bench. A woman puts her two sleeping children on the floor and throws a cloth over them. And we sit like a man scratching nothings with a stick in the sand and turning things over in his

mind. The home-made guitar twangs a no-tune in the
next carriage.

That night as I lay on the luggage rack after clearing
a space, rot crept into my sleep and my dreams were of
rottenness. I awoke and found that the smell of putre-
faction came not far from my head. I twisted and turned
in the limited space but the smell of rot was inescapable.
Sometimes the rot stopped, but just as I was about to
fall asleep it became clamorous and suffocated me awake.
In the morning my nostrils were parched and my throat
was sore.

We crossed the Zambezi at sunrise. Somewhere I had
read that the bridge across it was the longest in the world.
And the train trundled interminably over it, over large
tracts of sand. The channel was a mere trickle.

The old man pumped his primus stove in the corner of
the carriage and fetched water from the lavatory. His
enthusiasm for meat had not flagged. But when he dug
for it, the meat which had been blood-dripping red the
previous day had turned a sickly green and lively with
worms. He chopped it into small pieces, his head turned
to the window. I vowed that I would never eat that meat
even if I were dying of hunger. Mweli sat without saying a
word, his eyes fixed in front of him.

The old man took one bite of the soggy meat and his
mouth filled. He spat it out of the window and threw the
rest of the antelope after it.

As we approached the Nyasaland border my uneasiness
mounted. I had a feeling, a knowledge almost, that something terrible would happen. I turned to Mweli for
support.

'S'bali,' I said, 'I'm sure they'll see I'm not a Nyasa.'

'How? They don't care, S'bali, many people come and
go and nobody cares.'

But the fear persisted. It mounted as we crawled towards
Port Herald, the border. It mounted with heat and pros-

The old man took one bite of the soggy meat and his mouth filled

trated me. What if the Union Government had discovered
my flight? All it had to do was to set the telegraphs ticking
and the telephones ringing to the borders to cut off my
escape.

'Don't worry, S'bali. You've got your pass. Nothing will
happen.'

I had not said a word about escaping. Nobody had
asked me. And those who had been curious had supplied
their own answer: I was fetching gambling medicines
from Nyasaland.

Port Herald – the port of the blind. Swarms of blind
people came to meet the train. Starving children led them
and looked at us as they passed under the windows of the
train. Some of the blind people stood on the platform
scarcely facing the train, their lips moving continuously.
Flies clustered undisturbed around the edges of the
festering, weeping emptiness.

The heat mounted; piled up; attained a steady pitch.
The nostrils smelled their own blood. The fear inside me
prostrated me. Should I hide in the train? But I dragged
out my things from under the bench and from the rack
and staggered out into the battering sun. I formed
answers to questions I could not frame ... 'My father
went to the Union and died there ... Now I'm going to
grand-people ...'

The beggars crept behind us as we stood in two rows
facing one another. A muttering stole behind us; a muttering you could not escape. The muttering went on and on.
And when you thought it was over, that you had escaped,
another muttering stole up....

Nyasaland was determined to have its share of the
pickings. God knows we had already been picked to the
bone. Here there was organization; there was method.
A policeman snapped up the machados from our hands.
An African walked slowly up and down the line as if
he were inspecting a guard of honour and informed us

that he was the immigration officer and no one else. His word was final. We were cowed. I waited for the worst and could no longer frame answers and could not remember those I had framed.

'Don't worry, S'bali. It's just a bloody fool of a Nyasa . . .' It was good to have Mweli at my side.

It was a blitz. The immigration officer, receipt book in hand, walked from one policeman to the other. The policeman dug into the suitcases and brought out new things, or things that were suspectly whole. The immigration officer rushed up to the policeman. Men dipped into their purses for money. The officer wrote out a receipt and moved on. The old man came to us to look for change. He had been caught for four shillings and sixpence.

The policeman dug into my bag. He pulled out soiled things; battered things. He looked at me. I held my pass to him. He scattered things on the ground and rose. I thought I saw contempt in his eyes.

After the customs inspection came the smallpox vaccination. We bared our arms and a man came down the lines ploughing two furrows into them. Mweli shook his head. I smiled at him. It was over. I could enter Nyasaland; I had the authority to do so . . .

The short-handled hoe with the hump is the symbol of the south of Nyasaland. It bites into the ground which, when sown, brings forth food. For miles and miles men and women bared to the waist bend in the merciless sun. The hoe gallops in rhythmic strokes, in threes and sixes. The men and women turn and twist but the hoe gallops on and on; and on and on. The lands are studded with ant heaps into which the hoe cannot bite.

When we passed, the engine bellowed triumphantly, the hoes stopped galloping and backs straightened. People scraped the sweat from their faces, flicked it on to the ground and stared at us until we were far away. Then the backs bent and the faces came close to the earth and the hoes galloped, biting into the ground that when sown would bring food.

'Everything is grown by us,' said the old man with pride. 'We don't buy from Europeans.'

It grew furiously hot. We sweated gallons. We sat panting helplessly and one of our chaps became silly with the heat and the W.N.L.A. escort trussed his arms with a length of rope – not that he was any menace, though.

Some of our party had reached home. They got off at stations with names that are sweet to hear. They brushed themselves and coaxed their hats to something of their former shapes. They put on the airs of the city – or what they thought were the airs of the City of Gold of which they had seen nothing. But the journey had been too long and unkind. The finery, the initial finery was gone for ever.

The train grew hungry. We bought maize and chewed. We bought mpua (corn cakes), and munched them silently. We went to the lavatory and drank water till our stomachs filled. And passed Chiromo, Sankuleni, Tekerani . . .

Another engine joined the train. An Indian jumped out of the driver's cab to chat with the driver of the second engine. It had not been an African who had been driving the bellowing failure.

'I thought so, S'bali. I thought that something was wrong,' said the old man.

Mweli shook his head and looked at the old man out of his sick, tired eyes. 'A Nyasa is a Nyasa, S'bali . . .'

Then we began to climb. The engines pointed upwards and puffed and panted and bellowed. One engine had bellowed loud enough to wake the forest but two engines, set on out-bellowing each other, made the hills resound. And still up we went, climbing up gorges lined with trees that had reddish-brown leaves. We seemed headed for the skies.

Then a mountain block, a massif, ran in a soaring, jagged line to the north-west. It was brief, breath-taking, unbelievable. Then it was gone. And the engines still nosed to the sky. We rose higher and higher. The engines puffed and panted as they crawled up the hills. Then at Luchenza the engines levelled. We were at the top at last. In a few hours we should be in Blantyre. . . .

And now the mountain block which had soared and vanished reared in supreme majesty. It dwarfed everything else. We crawled under its gaze for miles and miles. The thickly clustering shadows continually shifted. The afternoon sun flashed on it. But some parts were already in sight.

The men leaned out of windows or sat with faces turned to the mountains. They sat for a long time. Then they turned away as in a sigh and started to talk of home and the people who would be waiting for them.

'Mlanje, S'bali . . . The mountain of Nyasaland,' said the old man. At that moment I suddenly realized how old he was. 'It's full of leopards, S'bali. . . .'

And the mountain seemed to say: 'I am. I was in old time. I will be old in new time. I am Mlanje. . . .'

At Limbe, while waiting for the train to Blantyre, six miles away, the symbol of the trail reared itself once more. Bundles rose to heads and shoulders and the wayfarers stood poised for the first steps of the shuffle. But whither at the end of the trail? Did they feel lost and restless without the symbol so that, long after its usefulness had gone, they went through the motions satisfying a need? The old man went to take his place in the single file. I sat on my things, Mweli at my side.

A policeman pointed at the line. And I just looked away, and kept looking away. Didn't he understand that the end was the end? Didn't he realize that the symbol had lost its purpose, that there was no journey at the journey's end? The symbol was irrelevant, a superstition . . .

I am sitting on the platform at Blantyre station and the lights have just snapped on. My 'cousins' haven't come for me yet and I will wait a little longer. I don't feel lost at all and the peace about me seems deep and abiding. Blantyre, Blantyre . . . How I have dreamt about you; how I have strained towards you. And now I am here. . . .

NOTES

Mtandizi: Rhodesian Native Labour Supply Commission. The name here given to the waiting-room

S'bali: brother-in-law, but here used as a term of familiarity

Khela: old man

tickey: three pence (a South African term)

mulatto: one of Afro-European ancestry

Goli: Johannesburg in South Africa

Tshini Mfondini: 'Gee, fellow'

machados: permit to enable Nyasas returning home to pass through Portuguese East Africa

W.N.L.A.: Witwatersrand Native Labour Association

City of Gold: Johannesburg

cousins: contacts who were to meet the author in Blantyre

Mzilikazi: recruited labour from the North now returning home after contract in the South African mines

EFUA SUTHERLAND

EFUA SUTHERLAND was born in Ghana and later studied at Cambridge. She became a teacher on her return and established a school in the Transvolta. She is essentially a poetess but writes prose as well. At present she is occupied with a school of drama connected in her native land with the University of Ghana. Her work has been broadcast on 'The Singing Net' a West African radio programme.

New Life at Kyerefaso is a prose poem. The plot is simple, concerning a stranger who marries Foruwa, the daughter of the Queen Mother, and through his zeal and physical work injects a new spirit into the village community. The villagers now have a new sense of purpose. Efua Sutherland's handling is beautiful and shows her poetic touch.

New Life at Kyerefaso

Shall we say
Shall we put it this way

Shall we say that the maid of Kyerefaso, Foruwa, daughter of the Queen Mother, was as young as a deer, graceful in limb? Such was she, with head held high, eyes soft and wide with wonder. And she was light of foot, light in all her moving.

Stepping springily along the water path like a deer that

had strayed from the thicket, springily stepping along the water path, she was a picture to give the eye a feast. And nobody passed her by but turned to look at her again.

Those of her village said that her voice in speech was like the murmur of a river quietly flowing beneath shadows of bamboo leaves. They said her smile would sometimes blossom like a lily on her lips and sometimes rise like sunrise.

The butterflies do not fly away from the flowers, they draw near. Foruwa was the flower of her village.

So shall we say

Shall we put it this way, that all the village butterflies, the men, tried to draw near her at every turn, crossed and crossed her path? Men said of her, 'She shall be my wife, and mine, and mine, and mine.'

But suns rose and set, moons silvered and died and as the days passed Foruwa grew more lovesome, yet she became no one's wife. She smiled at the butterflies and waved her hand lightly to greet them as she went swiftly about her daily work:

'Morning, Kweku,
Morning, Kwesi,
Morning, Kodwo,'
but that was all.

And so they said, even while their hearts thumped for her:

'Proud!
Foruwa is proud . . . and very strange.'

And so the men when they gathered would say:

'There goes a strange girl. She is not just stiff-in-the-neck proud, not just breasts-stuck-out-I-am-the-only-girl-in-the-village proud. What kind of pride is hers?'

The end of the year came round again, bringing the season of festivals. For the gathering in of corn, yams and cocoa there were harvest celebrations. There were

bride-meetings too. And it came to the time when the
Asafo companies should hold their festival. The village
was full of manly sounds, loud musketry and swelling
choruses.

The path-finding, path-clearing ceremony came to an
end. The Asafo marched on towards the Queen Mother's
house, the women fussing round them, prancing round
them, spreading their cloths in the way.

'Osee!' rang the cry. 'Osee!' to the manly men of old.
They crouched like leopards upon the branches.

Before the drums beat
Before the danger drums beat, beware!
Before the horns moaned
Before the wailing horns moaned, beware!

They were upright, they sprang. They sprang. They
sprang upon the enemy. But now, blood no more! No
more thundershot on thundershot.

But still we are the leopards on the branches. We are
those who roar and cannot be answered back. Beware, we
are they who cannot be answered back.

There was excitement outside the Queen Mother's
courtyard gate.

'Gently, gently,' warned the Asafo leader. 'Here comes
the Queen Mother.

'Spread skins of the gentle sheep in her way.
 Lightly, lightly walks our Mother Queen.
 Shower her with silver,
 Shower her with silver for she is peace.'

And the Queen Mother stood there, tall, beautiful,
before the men and there was silence.

'What news, what news do you bring?' she quietly
asked.

'We come with dusty brows from our path-finding,
Mother. We come with tired thorn-pricked feet. We come

D

to bathe in the coolness of your peaceful stream. We come to offer our manliness to new life.'

The Queen Mother stood there, tall and beautiful and quiet. Her fan-bearers stood by her and all the women clustered near. One by one the men laid their guns at her feet and then she said:

'It is well. The gun is laid aside. The gun's rage is silenced in the stream. Let your weapons from now on be your minds and your hands' toil.

'Come, maidens, women all, join the men in dance for they offer themselves to new life.'

There was one girl who did not dance.

'What, Foruwa!' urged the Queen Mother. 'Will you not dance? The men are tired of parading in the ashes of their grandfathers' glorious deeds. That should make you smile. They are tired of the empty croak: "We are men, we are men."

'They are tired of sitting like vultures upon the rubbish-heaps they have piled upon the half-built walls of their grandfathers. Smile, then, Foruwa, smile.

'Their brows shall now indeed be dusty, their feet thorn-pricked, and "I love my land" shall cease to be the empty croaking of a vulture upon the rubbish-heap. Dance, Foruwa, dance!'

Foruwa opened her lips and this was all she said: 'Mother, I do not find him here.'

'Who? Who do you not find here?'

'He with whom this new life shall be built. He is not here, Mother. These men's faces are empty; there is nothing in them, nothing at all.'

'Alas, Foruwa, alas, alas! What will become of you, my daughter?'

'The day I find him, Mother, the day I find the man, I shall come running to you, and your worries will come to an end.'

'But, Foruwa, Foruwa,' argued the Queen Mother,

although in her heart she understood her daughter, 'five years ago your rites were fulfilled. Where is the child of your womb? Your friend Maanan married. Your friend Esi married. Both had their rites with you.'

'Yes, Mother, they married and see how their steps once lively now drag in the dust. The sparkle has died out of their eyes. Their husbands drink palm wine the day long under the mango trees, drink palm wine and push counters across the draughtboards all the day, and are they not already looking for other wives? Mother, the man, I say, is not here.'

This conversation had been overheard by one of the men and soon others heard what Foruwa had said. That evening there was heard a new song in the village.

> 'There was a woman long ago,
> Tell that maid, tell that maid,
> There was a woman long ago,
> She would not marry Kwesi,
> She would not marry Kwaw,
> She would not, would not, would not.
> One day she came home with hurrying feet,
> I've found the man, the man, the man,
> Tell that maid, tell that maid,
> Her man looked like a chief,
> Tell that maid, tell that maid,
> Her man looked like a chief,
> Most splendid to see,
> But he turned into a python,
> He turned into a python
> And swallowed her up.'

From that time onward there were some in the village who turned their backs on Foruwa when she passed.

Shall we say
Shall we put it this way

Shall we say that a day came when Foruwa with hurrying feet came running to her mother? She burst through the courtyard gate; and there she stood in the courtyard, joy all over. And a stranger walked in after her and stood in the courtyard beside her, stood tall and strong as a pillar. Foruwa said to the astonished Queen Mother:

'Here he is, Mother, here is the man.'

The Queen Mother took a slow look at the stranger standing there strong as a forest tree, and she said:

'You carry the light of wisdom on your face, my son. Greetings, you are welcome. But who are you, my son?'

'Greetings, Mother,' replied the stranger quietly, 'I am a worker. My hands are all I have to offer your daughter, for they are all my riches. I have travelled to see how men work in other lands. I have that knowledge and my strength. That is all my story.'

Shall we say
Shall we put it this way,
strange as the story is, that Foruwa was given in marriage to the stranger.

There was a rage in the village and many openly mocked saying, 'Now the proud ones eat the dust.'

Yet shall we say
Shall we put it this way,
that soon, quite soon, the people of Kyerefaso began to take notice of the stranger in quite a different way.

'Who,' some said, 'is this who has come among us? He who mingles sweat and song, he for whom toil is joy and life is full and abundant?'

'See,' said the others, 'what a harvest the land yields under his ceaseless care.'

'He has taken the earth and moulded it into bricks. See what a home he has built, how it graces the village where it stands.'

'Look at the craft of his fingers, baskets or kente, stool or mat, the man makes them all.'

'And our children swarm about him, gazing at him with wonder and delight.'

Then it did not satisfy them any more to sit all day at their draughtboards under the mango trees.

'See what Foruwa's husband has done,' they declared; 'shall the sons of the land not do the same?'

And soon they began to seek out the stranger to talk with him. Soon they too were toiling, their fields began to yield as never before, and the women laboured joyfully to bring in the harvest. A new spirit stirred the village. As the carelessly built houses disappeared one by one, and new homes built after the fashion of the stranger's grew up, it seemed as if the village of Kyerefaso had been born afresh.

The people themselves became more alive and a new pride possessed them. They were no longer just grabbing from the land what they desired for their stomach's present hunger and for their present comfort. They were looking at the land with new eyes, feeling it in their blood, and thoughtfully building a permanent and beautiful place for themselves and their children.

'Osee!' It was festival-time again. 'Osee! Blood no more. Our fathers found for us the paths. We are the road-makers. They bought for us the land with their blood. We shall build it with our strength. We shall create it with our minds.'

Following the men were the women and children. On their heads they carried every kind of produce that the land had yielded and crafts that their fingers had created. Green plantains and yellow bananas were carried by the bunch in large white wooden trays. Garden eggs, tomatoes, red oil-palm nuts warmed by the sun were piled high in black earthen vessels. Oranges, yams, maize filled shining brass trays and golden calabashes. Here and there were children proudly carrying colourful mats, baskets and toys which they themselves had made.

The Queen Mother watched the procession gathering on the new village playground now richly green from recent rains. She watched the people palpitating in a massive dance towards her where she stood with her fan-bearers outside the royal house. She caught sight of Foruwa. Her load of charcoal in a large brass tray which she had adorned with red hibiscus danced with her body. Happiness filled the Queen Mother when she saw her daughter thus.

Then she caught sight of Foruwa's husband. He was carrying a white lamb in his arms, and he was singing happily with the men. She looked on him with pride. The procession had approached the royal house.

'See!' rang the cry of the Asafo leader, 'See how the best in all the land stands. See how she stands waiting, our Queen Mother. Waiting to wash the dust from our brows in the coolness of her peaceful stream. Spread skins of the gentle sheep in her way, gently, gently. Spread the yield of the land before her. Spread the craft of your hands before her, gently, gently.

'Lightly, lightly walks our Queen Mother, for she is peace.'

NOTE

kente : a kind of cloth

JONATHAN KARIARA

JONATHAN KARIARA is a Kikuyu from Kenya, and, after being educated locally, went to the University College of Makerere in Uganda, where he took an honours degree in English. Since then he has been on the staff of the East African Literature Bureau in Nairobi.

In this story Jonathan Kariara sketches the relationship between his grandmother and father. He, who had been a great Kikuyu warrior, had now degenerated to cooking for himself, and she, from a proud woman formerly flouting tradition, now becomes one 'who watches her girlhood dance on the horizon.'

Her Warrior

She was a tall woman with high cheekbones, now more emphasized than ever by the loss of her molar teeth. Her lips were finer than most of her tribe's and wore a shut, rather sour expression. Her eyes seemed to be always fixed on the distance, as though she didn't 'see' or mind the immediate, but dwelt in the eternal. She was not like other children's grandmothers we knew, who would spoil their grandchildren and had their huts 'just outside the hedge' of their sons' homesteads. Grandmother lived three hills away, which was inexplicable.

All the other grandmothers had some relationship with their ageing husbands. Some had strange dreams of how their dead ones had visited them in their dreams, and would repeat their last night's experience in great detail, time and time again, thus relieving the monotony of their existence. There was Grandma Wacu who was always rescuing her husband from toppling into the fire as he dozed and would scold him with a mighty wrath in spite of her neighbours' constant protestations that her husband was stone deaf. There were the 'Lizards,' so called for their daylong basking in the sun. Their life now consisted of following the course of the sun; outside their respective huts in the morning, under the Mukoigo tree at noon, at the back of their huts at sunset, taking in the last rays of the sun. There was Gacucu (Little Grandmother) who after forty years of married life was still having fights with her husband, and indiscriminately would tell her troubles in great detail to us children, to our great joy but so much to the embarrassment of her married daughters.

Grandmother was different. She never mentioned her husband. If ever she heard any of us refer to him she would instantly snort and push away any small object near her with an impatient sweep of her long arm. If any of us dared ask her why she never mentioned him she would instantly lose her temper and like a broody hen ruffling her feathers would rise to gather her few possessions, for a return journey to her hut three hills away. She had been insulted.

On this occasion, though, she had been asked to come, to see him. He was dying. 'Tell her she must come,' my father had told the man he sent to her. When she arrived she was greatly changed. She who before had walked with such a firm step for her age, who had such a haughty face, was now in a state of nervous excitement. My mother hurried to meet her at the gate as she arrived. 'You must see ...' 'See what?' snapped Grandmother, pushing her aside and confronting my father. 'And so I must come, Karanja. So I'm wanted now?' she almost jeered. He, fearing she might say something which would sorrow both for the rest of their lives, left the house immediately and left Mother to face the old woman. 'Who wants me here?' she demanded, stamping here and there with a stick like a blind man 'looking' for his way. 'Who wants me here?' she repeated. We had always enjoyed her tantrums before, we knew they always ended in her either shortening her visit to us, or in a wonderful mood when simply and vividly she would tell us strange stories of her adventures as a girl, before she married. But now it was different, although she was raving, her mind was not on what she was saying, rather she was like a receiver of bad news who puts off the announcement with gibberish. She kept on looking furtively in the direction of his hut, and Mother, guessing what was worrying her, had to break the news she feared. 'He is not there. We persuaded him to go to the mission hospital, Mother,' she said. For a few seconds the other woman was like somebody choking. She gasped and swayed and would have fallen unconscious had Mother not done what was very unexpected of her. She who always feared the older woman rushed to where she was standing and gripped her by the shoulders, turning Grandmother to face her. Steadily she gazed into Grandmother's face, as though searching for a clue that would thaw the cold resentment the old woman had built up towards her husband. And her eyes also seemed to accuse the older woman, as if saying, 'You too were responsible, even to sending him to the mission hospital.' The other woman might have understood her for she did not rave now but was leaning on Mother, helplessly. Mother took her into the house.

This is the story as we came to learn later. They married 'outside the tribe'. That means, she saw her man and decided in her heart to marry him. He saw her heart's decision, and quietly but finally accepted it. Thus they disregarded all the tribal forms of courting and marriage and let it be known they were going to marry. She simply told her parents she was marrying him, so wounding their pride in the implication that they did not count, tribal customs did not count. A girl must not decide for herself finally whom she is going to marry. But she was marrying Wanyoike, the great warrior, so their pride was partly mollified. He on the other hand could have chosen any bride he wanted to marry. He was a war leader, a great but short-lived war leader.

They were not married for long when the Masai declared war on the Kikuyu. They had cunningly chosen their moment, for the Kikuyus had just been through a period of famine and were rather weakened. Anger that the Masai should so cunningly involve them, when it was usual for them to be the cunning party, gave them greater courage than they normally possessed when fighting the dreaded Maitha.

The war was fought and the Kikuyu were being driven from hill to hill. Wanyoike, one of the Kikuyu leaders, was blind with anger. For days he had fought, never uttering a word, but as the conviction grew that they would lose the battle his anger grew into such a frenzied hatred of the Masai that he would do anything to see them retreat. Next day he did the unexpected, the unprecedented. He gripped the long arm of a Kikuyu warrior who had fallen dead beside him and chopped it off at the shoulder blade. His living hand gripped the dead one and, waving it aloft, he charged into a group of Masai warriors, striking right and left with the dead man's arm. At first they did not understand what was happening, until one after the other they felt the clammy touch of the dead arm. Then they saw. And fear spread among them, a primeval fear of warm blood coming in contact with the disintegrating dead. One after the other they let out a cry, the inhuman cry of a trapped wild animal. It spread like fire with a wind behind it; it echoed in every warrior, Kikuyu or Masai, so that the Kikuyu paused, paralysed with fear, and the Masai, afraid of 'evil-let-loose', took to flight. Seeing them flee the Kikuyu fell to, and made history that day for grandmothers to repeat to their grandchildren of the day the Masai were wholly defeated. But it was curious that not one of them mentioned Wanyoike who caused the victory. To them as to the defeated Masai it was greatly shocking, therefore taboo, that the living blood in a man should so dare to come into such close contact with the dead.

Wanyoike came back from a war a lonely man. Once the victory was won they were all afraid of him. Deadly afraid. Many of them said later that they all wanted to be religiously cleansed after that battle, although they should have been singing victorious. They hurried on to their respective huts, who should have come back one body, united in and drunk with victory. Wanyoike crept back to his young wife, afraid of himself. So she took to protecting him, fiercely. 'The battle she fought!' the old women in the village would say. 'You did not dare ask her how the child she was carrying kicked. It was Wanyoike's so what interest could you have in it? We never knew the little things she liked during her time of waiting. She was proud and foolish and had a way of making you look just like a shrivelled leaf floating on the wind, with a wave of her hand. You did not dare show up at her house. "What do you want?" she would demand, sweeping out like a mad thing, even though you might have been carrying anointing oil to her. When the child arrived she had "no woman with her".' Then they would add with a shudder: 'Some people think he helped her with the birth of the child.'

When the child was a few days old Wanyoike killed a fat ram and invited his relations to come and meet the 'new guest' arrived. There was no beer at the feast, for

his wife would not agree to the feasting and said she
would rather go through what she had recently been
through than debase herself by asking any of those women
to help her with beer making. So the feast Wanyoike
provided never came to life, for not even birds can sing
on dry throats. The party was rather flagging when she
came out. 'You should have seen her fury, that their
relations should come to bless the child! And she would
not eat the meat, would not touch her special portion,
but went about like a sheep suffering from lock-jaw. We
had all sympathized with her in the past but now we
were not sorry to see that her husband was very angry
with her, and we knew what his anger meant. It was
then that their fights started. She would bow to no man,
but would lift her long strong arms and with fury would
strike. He would get hold of her and shake her until there
was no wind in her. And they are the ones who had walked
together in the cool of the evening, as no other woman
dare with her husband. Their fights were still and terrible,
like quicksands, each keen to destroy the other. Then one
day he decided they could not live together and soon
after built her a hut where she now lives. He never called
her back but something went out of him with her de-
parture. He quickly grew old and started cooking for
himself, ay, one of our warriors ended cooking for himself!'

Mother must have succeeded in persuading Grandmother to see her dying husband. 'What are we waiting
for, then?' we heard her demand of Mother impatiently.
Soon they were outside, ready to go to the hospital. But
she was not destined to see her husband any more. As
they came out at the door my father came in at the gate.
Something in his face must have broken the news to the
women. Grandmother looked steadily in his face and
something, as it were, snapped in the very core of her
being. She did not break down in weeping as many

women would have done. She simply turned to pick the
little bag she always carried which had fallen when she
saw my father. 'It is well,' she said, 'that I did not see
him in those ridiculous things they give them to wear at
the hospital. I would never have forgiven him if I had
seen him in those – those ...' She could not continue
but walked to the gate. And as she fumbled to open it
she was no longer a proud old lady. She was a tottering
old woman who would from now on sit outside her hut,
looking at the horizon. 'She is watching her girlhood
dance in the horizon,' her neighbours would say if they
saw her sitting thus. But most of the time she saw nothing,
nothing.

PETER CLARKE

PETER CLARKE was born in Simonstown, near Cape Town, in 1929. After attending Livingstone High School he went to work in the local dockyard as a ship's painter. Later he decided to become a full-time artist and after many exhibitions he was awarded a grant to study at the Rijksmuseum Akademie in Amsterdam. As a writer he won the *Drum* short story competition. The story below, *Eleven o'clock: The Wagons, the Shore* won a prize in the *Encounter* literary competition in 1958, and was subsequently broadcast by the B.B.C.

This story describes eleven o'clock at a primary school in South Africa. Eleven o'clock brings a fifteen-minute break and the pupils in Simonstown go down to the sea, sit alongside the derelict wagons on the beach, munch their lunches and watch the seagulls. They can differentiate between the birds sufficiently well to recognize and name them. Peter Clarke describes this eleven o'clock break during different seasons of the year.

Eleven o'clock: The Wagons,
The Shore

The old brown framework of the wagons stood like the stark, decrepit remains of naked, dismembered corpses on the edge of the Bus Company's property overlooking the shore. Here at eleven o'clock I sat down with cousin

Albert, Boeta and the other big boys, 'Happy' Thompson, Jeffy, 'Ballie' and Dicky. Sometimes the gang members changed but I was always the youngest and the smallest of the mob sitting on the wagons. Then I delighted in the company and knowledge of people older than myself.

As soon as the bell rang for the fifteen minutes' break we made a dash out of the backyard gate, up the back lane, past Shannon's house, which was a converted shop, and past the old Phoenix Hall and then down the wide drive-way, past the windows of the Masonic Club and the Villa Zain, with the tall palm in its garden opposite the huge bus garage, until we crossed the open gravel front to the line of wagons.

The wagons were formerly the property of old Albertyn who had a cartage concern down-town. When the wagons were unfit for further use he had dumped them on the foreshore where they were left to the mercy of time and the elements, until they became so battered that they just fell apart through utter weariness from the unevenness of the battle.

Old Albertyn's house stood on the edge of the shore almost surrounded by its big garden, which was densely overcrowded with plants and trees growing in wild confusion and disorder, giving it a somewhat mysterious appearance from whichever side one looked at it. The garden was dominated by tall blue-gums which cast a perpetual shade over the place, making each tree assume a gloomy, sulky mood of unhappiness in the sepia and olive-green shadows. Only when a strong wind blew the sea's expanse into hundreds of restless waves, which the white sea horses rode on, up and down, up and down, and the sky into masses of dark grey and blue rainclouds and whipped the beach sand up over the wagons and the dust along the gravel front, only then did those trees appear to be gay. Then the stiff cypresses lifted up their heavy green foliage and the oleanders along the fence

shook their cake-pink and ivory-white flowers and waxy
leaves to and fro, to and fro, and the banana palms
clashed their torn leaves against each other and against
the branches of other trees, noisy like a noisy child, glad
for the wind that came up off the sea like a small hurricane
and gave it a voice, while the long yellow rods of bamboo
that were tipped with leaves like green daggers, swayed
and swayed from side to side, up, down, up, down, its
humble sideways creak soft beneath the groans and sighs
of the blue-gums. When the wind ran through the corners
of that garden beneath those trees and between those
bushy plants it stole scenty fragrances from each plant,
particularly the roses and oleanders, and tossed it to us
and anybody willing to wait along its fences to smell
them.

We sat on the tattered remains of the wagons, rocking
to and fro in the wind, munching the eleven o'clock slices
of 'tuppenny' loaves, feeling them become doughy and
'gooey' as they mixed with spittle, butter and apricot jam,
hesitating on the brink of the throat into which they sank
unwillingly with each difficult swallow.

Along the edge of the crumpled bread-paper the sea
licked, spat and spumed, depositing foam and seaweed
and old bread and broken planks. Off the shore-line the
fishing boats tugged restlessly at their anchors and over
the dock-wall we could see the big warships greyly riding
at attention.

With our hands clutching the splintered side-beams of
our wagons, we let our eyes follow along the white flight
of seagulls as they swept along the alleys of the sky-lanes,
sweeping, banking, hovering, swooping down to collect
juicy tit-bits of soggy bread and swollen orange, and when
these showed promise of nothing they sat and waited ex-
pectantly with the patience of a reception committee on the
end of the sanitation pipe, until at long intervals it poured
off dribbles of refuse. Then they dropped their white fig-

bodies into the tossing waters, bundling each other out of the way, so as to peck at the morsels they fancied to be the best.

We and other schoolboys called them 'skollyboys' because they were always 'skollying' for something to eat. But the wagon kids were the only boys who tried to recognize certain gulls every day. Sometimes we succeeded and then we watched our particular 'Joey' or 'Pat' or 'Bill' flying about until bored with his surroundings he would let a finger of wind lift him under each wing-tip and transport him on a fast, smooth ride towards the town pier, the fishing boats, the big yachts, the tugs and over the black iron boundary fence of the old dockyard, while our minds whispered furiously, 'Good-bye Joe, good-bye Joe, see you tomorrow again', as our bird flew away and the distance changed it into a tiny white speck. Then there was always tomorrow and the bell . . .

When the days were wintry and eleven o'clock dry, we leant on the weathered timbers of the wagons and watched the mists of distant rains flushing the faces of the coastal mountains, hugging the outline of the bay, washing out the colour of mountain, sea and sky the way water washes out the tints of a delicate watercolour painting; coming nearer and nearer until, running hard for shelter, we felt it licking at our heels. Those were far, far rains and we wondered if they had come to us all the way from the forests and jungles of the Equator. Watching, you could see it miles and miles away up country as it came along and it made one wonder.

Sometimes, smack in the middle of winter, we got a clear day with an icy nip on its edge, sharp, like the sharp point of a knife gently prodding the palm of the hand. On those 'turned-up-collar' days, with hands stuck deep in pockets and taste of bread and sugary toffee in mouths, we stood on the beach and looked across, over the fortress forms of Royal Navy ships, to the blue mountains far

'Good-bye Joe, good-bye Joe, see you tomorrow again!'

away on the other side of the bay, their peaks and crests and ravines dazzling white and dusty blue with a fall of snow. Then we became envious. 'It would be nice if snow fell in the peninsula for a change, then we could have real snow-fights. Pity though, there would be sand on the snowballs if we battled in the school-yard,' said cousin Albert.

There was just a chance after the eleven o'clock bread, the wagons, and toes in the sea, to run between buildings to have a quick look at the horses in Albertyn's stables and the blacksmith next door. We knew those horses because after school we saw them in the street pulling the loaded wagons through the town and when they stopped the driver allowed us to touch them, which we did with the tips of our timid fingers.

The blacksmith's shop, with its excessive heat and bright, fiery red and pitch, pitch black and hard brown iron that was changed into white-hot iron, was always a source of delight. Our wonder made it a place of magic and the blacksmith a magician. But one day he shouted at us as we stood in the doorway and was turned into an ordinary man of ordinary flesh and blood and muscle with the vagaries of an ordinary human temperament. And we ran from reality, back to school, past the back windows of the garage in which the bulky bodies of the buses slumbered, elephant-like, in the deep gloominess because in the distance we could hear the bell . . .

In the warm months of the first butterflies, we watched the daisies lightly sprinkling themselves, white and lemon and orange, between the sharp blades of grass in the lee of the petrified springs and rusted iron bands of the wagon timbers. Between poles the red hands of fishermen blooded thin cords of black fishline the length of the grassy beach and, half-way up the sand, stink barnacles fell from the edge of scrapers, off the hulls of snoek vessels home from the Walvis Bay coast's winter fishing. The dark holds of

those vessels had borne dried snoek, stacked one on top
of the other, their flayed bodies stiff with the glittering
crystal-like salt; and bulging bags of delicious 'butter-pits'
garnered from the insides of a melon of the hot South
West Africa desert-land. When the snoek-catchers came
home after the winter's fishing the boys of the mission
school sat in class and cracked the husks of the 'pits' while
the grumpy schoolmaster had his back turned.

On the warmer days we explored the territories left
vacant by the ebb-tide and caught the small grey-brown
and grey-black mottled rockfish known in our home
language as 'Klipvissies'. Some of the larger of those fish,
caught in the rock pools with a penny hook tied to a
piece of tough string, found their way into frying-pans
and were eaten at supper-time. And when the wind put
tight fingers between the rocks and pushed the tide up
into our pools we retreated to the dryness of higher ground
and listened to the rasping voice of the date-palm, in the
garden of the Villa Zain, clattering its dagger-leaved
branches together outside the tightly closed windows of
the white and green villa.

Those were far, far days and now it is all over. Time
has taken many hours and changed them into the past.
Bare-footed schoolboys grew up and became men, and
the wagons disappeared beneath the reclaimed land of
a new foreshore. Only the sea and the wind remain. Now
when the sea roars and the wind rises up off the water,
and, dashing through the corners of old Albertyn's garden,
makes every plant and tree rejoice, then my heart goes
back to those far-off eleven o'clock days of the wagons
and the sea.

NOTES

skollyboys: young ruffians
snoek: a local, very tasty fish

LUIS BERNARDO HONWANA

Luis Bernardo Honwana was born in the city of Lourenço Marques, Mozambique, in 1942. The second of eight children, he attended the local primary school in Moamba, and returned to Lourenço Marques for his High School education. His career was interrupted for two years when he had to go out to work, owing to financial difficulties in the family. He is now in his seventh year of High School, and will shortly be continuing his studies at the University. At present he studies part-time and works as a journalist on *Diario de Mozambique* and *Voz Africana*. *Papa, the snake and I*, is one of a collection of his stories which has just been published in Lourenço Marques.

This is a charming story set in a small village in Mozambique where we see the events of an ordinary day as they occur and appear to a boy. We meet his mother, the pillar of the family, who barks her commands in both Ronga and Portuguese, the less aggressive father, his brothers and sisters, and the girl, Sartina. Mr Castro is an arrogant local Portuguese, quick to demand retribution for any loss or imagined insult. But the main characters in this story are the snake and the dog Toto.

Papa, the Snake and I

As soon as Papa left the table to read the newspaper in the sitting-room, I got up as well. I knew that Mama and the others would take a while longer, but I didn't feel like staying with them at all.

Just as I stood up, Mama looked at me and said, 'Come here, let me look at your eyes.'

I went towards her slowly, because when Mama calls us we never know whether she's cross or not. After she had lifted my lids with the index finger of her left hand to make a thorough examination, she looked down at her plate and I stood waiting for her to send me away or to say something. She finished chewing, swallowed, and picked up the bone in her fingers to peep through the cavity, shutting one eye. Then she turned to me suddenly with a bewildered look on her face.

'Your eyes are bloodshot, you're weak and you've lost your appetite.'

The way she spoke made me feel obliged to say that none of this was my fault or else that I didn't do it on purpose. All the others looked on very curiously to see what was going to happen.

Mama peered down the middle of the bone again. Then she began to suck it, shutting her eyes, and only stopped for a moment to say, 'Tomorrow you're going to take a laxative.'

The moment the others heard this, they began eating again very quickly and noisily. Mama didn't seem to have anything else to say, so I went out into the yard.

It was hot everywhere, and I could see no one on the road. Over the back wall three oxen gazed at me. They must have come back from the water trough at the Administration and stayed to rest in the shade. Far away, over the oxen's horns, the grey tufts of the dusty thorn trees trembled like flames. Everything vibrated in the distance, and heat waves could even be seen rising from the stones in the road. Sartina was sitting on a straw mat in the shade of the house, eating her lunch. Chewing slowly, she looked around, and from time to time, with a careless gesture, she shooed away the fowls who came close to her hoping for crumbs. Even so, every now and then one of the bolder ones would jump on to the edge of the plate and run off with a lump of mealie meal in its beak, only to be pursued by the others. In their wild dispute, the lump became so broken up that in the end even the smallest chicken would get its bit to peck.

When she saw me coming near, Sartina pulled her capulana down over her legs, but she kept her hand spread out in front of her knees, firmly convinced that I wanted to peep at something, and when I looked away she still didn't move her hand.

Toto came walking along slowly with his tongue hanging out, and went to the place where Sartina was sitting. He sniffed the plate from afar and turned away, taking himself off to the shade of the wall where he looked for a soft place to lie down. When he found one, he curled round with his nose almost on his tail, and only lay still when his stomach touched the ground. He gave a long yawn, and dropped his head between his paws. He wriggled a little, making sure that he was in the most comfortable position, then covered his ears with his paws.

When she had finished eating, Sartina looked at me insistently before removing her hand which covered the space between her knees, and only when she was sure I was not looking did she spring to her feet with a jump. The plate was so clean that it shone, but after darting a last suspicious glance at me, she took it to the trough. She moved languidly, swaying from the waist as her hips rose and fell under her capulana. She bent over the trough, but the backs of her legs were exposed in this position, so she went to the other side for me not to see.

Mama appeared at the kitchen door, still holding the bone in her hand and, before calling Sartina to clear the table, she looked around to see if everything was in order. 'Don't forget to give Toto his food,' she said in Ronga.

Sartina went inside, drying her hands on her capulana, and afterwards came out with a huge pile of plates. When she came out the second time she brought the tablecloth and shook it on the stairs. While the fowls were skirmishing for the crumbs, pecking and squawking at each other, she folded it in two, four, and eight, and then went back inside. When she came out again she brought the aluminium plate with Toto's food, and put it on the cement cover of the water meter. Toto didn't have to be called to eat and even before the plate was put down, he threw himself on his food. He burrowed into the pile of rice with his nose, searching for the bits of meat, which he gulped up greedily as he found them. When no meat was left, he pushed the bones aside and ate some rice. The fowls were all around him, but they didn't dare to come nearer because they knew very well what Toto was like when he was eating.

When he had swallowed the rice, Toto pretended he didn't want any more and went to sit in the shade of the sugar-cane, waiting to see what the fowls would do. They came nervously towards his food, and risked a peck or two, very apprehensively. Toto watched this without making a single movement. Encouraged by the passivity of the dog, the fowls converged on the rice with great enthusiasm, creating an awful uproar. It was then that Toto threw himself on the heap, pawing wildly in all directions and growling like an angry lion. When the fowls disappeared, fleeing to all corners of the yard, Toto went back to the shade of the sugar-cane, waiting for them to gather together again.

Before going to work Papa went to look at the chicken run with Mama. They both appeared at the kitchen door, Mama already wearing her apron and Papa with a toothpick in his mouth and his newspaper under his arm. When they passed me Papa was saying, 'It's impossible, it's impossible, things can't go on like this.'

I went after them, and when we entered the chicken run Mama turned to me as if she wanted to say something, but then she changed her mind and went towards the wire netting. There were all sorts of things piled up behind the chicken run: pipes left over from the building of the windmill on the farm, blocks which were bought when Papa was still thinking of making outhouses of cement, boxes, pieces of wood, and who knows what else. The fowls sometimes crept in amongst these things and laid their eggs where Mama couldn't reach them. On one side of the run lay a dead fowl, and Mama pointed to it and said, 'Now there's this one, and I don't know how many others have just died from one day to the next. The chickens simply disappear, and the eggs too. I had this one left here for you to see. I'm tired of talking to you about this, and you still don't take any notice.'

'All right, all right, but what do you want me to do about it?'

'Listen, the fowls die suddenly, and the chickens disappear. No one goes into the chicken run at night, and we've never heard any strange noise. You must find out what's killing the fowls and chickens.'

'What do you think it is?'

'The fowls are bitten and the chickens are eaten. It can only be the one thing you think it is – if there are any thoughts in your head.'

'All right, tomorrow I'll get the snake killed. It's Sunday, and it will be easy to get people to do it. Tomorrow.'

Papa was already going out of the chicken run when Mama said, now in Portuguese, 'But tomorrow without fail, because I don't want any of my children bitten by a snake.'

Papa had already disappeared behind the corner of the house on his way to work when Mama turned to me and said, 'Haven't you ever been taught that when your father and mother are talking you shouldn't stay and listen? My children aren't usually so bad-mannered. Who do you take after?'

She turned on Sartina, who was leaning against the wire netting and listening. 'What do you want? Did anyone call you? I'm talking to my son and it's none of your business.'

Sartina couldn't have grasped all that because she didn't understand Portuguese very well, but she drew away from the netting, looking very embarrassed, and went to the trough again. Mama went on talking to me, 'If you think you'll fool me and take the gun to go hunting you're making a big mistake. Heaven help you if you try to do a thing like that! I'll tan your backside for you! And if you think you'll stay here in the chicken run you're also mistaken. I don't feel like putting up with any of your nonsense, d'you hear?'

Mama must have been very cross, because for the whole day I hadn't heard her laugh as she usually did. After talking to me she went out of the chicken run and I followered her. When she passed Sartina, she asked her in Ronga, 'Is it very hot under your capulana? Who told you to come here and show your legs to everybody?'

Sartina said nothing, walked round the trough, and went on washing the plates, bending over the other side.

Mama went away and I went to sit where I had been before. When Sartina saw me she turned on me resentfully, threw me a furious glance, and went round the trough again. She began to sing a monotonous song, one of those songs of hers that she sometimes spent the whole afternoon singing over and over again when she was angry.

Toto was bored with playing with the fowls, and had already finished eating his rice. He was sleeping again with his paws over his ears. Now and then he rolled himself in the dust and lay on his back with his legs folded in the air.

It was stiflingly hot, and I didn't know whether I'd go

hunting as I usually did every Saturday, or if I'd go to the chicken run to see the snake.

Madunana came into the yard with a pile of firewood on his back, and went to put it away in the corner where Sartina was washing the plates. When she saw him, she stopped singing and tried to manage an awkward smile.

After looking all around, Madunana pinched Sartina's bottom, and she gave an embarrassed giggle and responded with a sonorous slap on his arm. The two of them laughed happily together without looking at each other.

Just then, Nandito, Joãozinho, Nelita and Gita ran out after a ball, and started kicking it around the yard with great enjoyment.

Mama came to the kitchen door, dressed up to go out. As soon as she appeared, Madunana bent down quickly to the ground, pretending to look for something, and Sartina bent over the trough.

'Sartina, see if you can manage not to break any plates before you finish. Hurry up. You, Madunana, leave Sartina alone and mind your own business. I don't want any of that nonsense here. If you carry on like this I'll tell the boss.

'You, Ginho,' (now she spoke in Portuguese) 'look after the house and remember you're not a child any more. Don't hit anybody and don't let the children go out of the yard. Tina and Lolota are inside clearing up – don't let them get up to mischief.

'Sartina,' (in Ronga) 'when you've finished with that put the kettle on for the children's tea and tell Madunana to go and buy bread. Don't let the children finish the whole packet of butter.

'Ginho,' (now in Portuguese) 'look after everything – I'm coming back just now. I'm going along to Aunty Lucia's for a little chat.'

Mama straightened her dress and looked around to see
if everything was in order, then went away.

Mr Castro's dog, Wolf, was watching Toto from the
street. As soon as he saw Wolf, Toto ran towards him and
they started to bark at each other.

All the dogs of the village were frightened of Toto, and
even the biggest of them ran away when he showed his
temper. Toto was small, but he had long white hair
which bristled up like a cat's when he was angry, and this is
what must have terrified the other dogs.

Usually he kept away from them, preferring to enter-
tain himself with the fowls – even bitches he only tolerated
at certain times. For me he was a dog with a 'pedigree' or
at least 'pedigree' could only mean the qualities he possessed. He had an air of authority, and the only person he
feared was Mama, although she had never hit him. Just
to take him off a chair we had to call her because he
snarled and showed his teeth even at Papa.

The two dogs were face to face, and Wolf had already
started to retreat, full of fear. At this moment Dr Reis's
dog, Kiss, passed by, and Toto started to bark at him too.
Kiss fled at once, and Wolf pursued him, snapping at his
hind quarters, only leaving him when he was whining with
pain. When Wolf came back to Toto they immediately
made friends and began playing together.

Nandito came and sat down next to me, and told me,
without my asking, that he was tired of playing ball.

'So why have you come here?'

'Don't you want me to?'

'I didn't say that.'

'Then I'll stay.'

'Stay if you like.'

I got up and he followed me. 'Where are you going?
Are you going hunting?'

'No.'

'Well then?'

'Stop pestering me. I don't like talking to kids.'

'You're also a kid. Mama still hits you.'

'Say that again and I'll bash your face in.'

'All right, I won't say it again.'

I went into the chicken run and he came after me. The pipes were hot, and I had to move them with a cloth. The dust that rose was dense and suffocating.

'What are you looking for? Shall I help you?'

I began to move the blocks one by one and Nandito did the same. 'Get away!'

He went to the other end of the run and began to cry.

When I had removed the last block of the pile I saw the snake. It was a mamba, very dark in colour. When it realized it had been discovered it wound itself up more tightly and lifted its triangular head. Its eyes shone vigilantly and its black forked tongue quivered menacingly.

I drew back against the fence, then sat down on the ground. 'Don't cry, Nandito.'

'You're nasty. You don't want to play with me.'

'Don't cry any more. I'll play with you just now. Don't cry.'

We both sat quietly. The little head of the snake came slowly to rest on the topmost coil, and the rest of its body stopped trembling. But it continued to watch me attentively.

'Nandito, say something, talk to me . . .'

'What do you want me to say?'

'Anything you like.'

'I don't feel like saying anything.'

Nandito was still rubbing his eyes and feeling resentful towards me.

'Have you ever seen a snake? Do you like snakes? Are you scared of them? Answer me!'

'Where are the snakes?' Nandito jumped up in terror and looked around.

'In the bush. Sit down and talk.'

'Aren't there any snakes here?'

'No. Talk. Talk to me about snakes.'

Nandito sat down very close to me.

'I'm very frightened of snakes. Mama says it's dangerous to go out in the bush because of them. When we're walking in the grass we can step on one by mistake and get bitten. When a snake bites us we die. Sartina says that if a snake bites us and we don't want to die we must kill it, burn it 'till it's dry then eat it. She says she's already eaten a snake, so she won't die even if she gets bitten.'

'Have you ever seen a snake?'

'Yes, in Chico's house. The servant killed it in the chicken run.'

'What was it like?'

'It was big and red, and it had a mouth like a frog.'

'Would you like to see a snake now?'

Nandito got up and leaned against me fearfully. 'Is there a snake in the chicken run? I'm scared – let's get out.'

'If you want to get out, go away. I didn't call you to come in here.'

'I'm frightened to go alone.'

'Then sit here until I feel like going out.'

The two of us stayed very quietly for a while.

Toto and Wolf were playing outside the fence. They were running from one post to another, going all the way round and starting again. At every post they raised a leg and urinated.

Then they came inside the chicken run and lay on their stomachs to rest. Wolf saw the snake immediately and began to bark. Toto barked as well, although he had his back turned towards it.

'Brother, are there always snakes in every chicken run?'

'No.'

'Is there one in here?'

'Yes.'

'Well then, why don't we go out? I'm scared!'

'Go out if you want to – go on!'

Wolf advanced towards the snake, barking more and more frenziedly. Toto turned his head, but still did not realize what was wrong.

Wolf's legs were trembling and he pawed the ground in anguish. Now and again he looked at me uncomprehendingly, unable to understand why I did not react to his hysterical alarm. His almost human eyes were filled with panic.

'Why is he barking like that?'

'Because he's seen the snake.'

The mamba was curled up in the hollow between some blocks, and it unwound its body to give itself the most solid support possible. Its head and the raised neck remained poised in the air, unaffected by the movement of the rest of its body. Its eyes shone like fires.

Wolf's appeals were now horribly piercing, and his hair was standing up around his neck.

Leaning against the fence, Tina and Lolota and Madunana looked on curiously.

'Why don't you kill the snake?' Nandito's voice was very tearful and he was clutching me around the neck.

'Because I don't feel like it.'

The distance between the snake and the dog was about five feet. However, the snake had inserted its tail in the angle formed between a block and the ground, and had raised its coils one by one, preparing for the strike. The triangular head drew back imperceptibly, and the base of the lifted neck came forward. Seeming to be aware of the proximity of his end, the dog began to bark even more frantically, without, however, trying to get away from the snake. From a little way behind, Toto, now on his feet as well, joined in the barking.

For a fraction of a second the neck of the snake curved while the head leaned back. Then, as if the tension of its pliant body had snapped a cord that fastened its head to the ground, it shot forward in a lightning movement impossible to follow. Although the dog had raised himself on his hind legs like a goat, the snake struck him full on the chest. Free of support, the tail of the snake whipped through the air, reverberating with the movement of the last coil.

Wolf fell on his back with a suppressed whine, pawing convulsively. The mamba abandoned him immediately, and with a spring disappeared between the pipes.

'A Nhoka!' screamed Sartina.

Nandito threw me aside and ran out of the chicken run with a yell, collapsing into the arms of Madunana. As soon as he felt free of the snake, Wolf vanished in half a dozen leaps in the direction of Mr Castro's house.

The children all started to cry without having understood what had happened. Sartina took Nandito to the house, carrying him in her arms. Only when the children disappeared behind Sartina did I call Madunana to help me kill the snake.

Madunana waited with a cloth held up high while I moved the pipes with the aid of a broomstick. As soon as the snake appeared Madunana threw the cloth over it, and I set to beating the heap with my stick.

When Papa came back from work Nandito had come round from the shock, and was weeping copiously. Mama, who had not yet been to see the snake, went with Papa to the chicken run. I went there as well, and saw Papa turn the snake over on to its back with a stick.

'I don't like to think of what a snake like this could have done to one of my children.' Papa smiled. 'Or to anyone else. It was better this way. What hurts me is to think that these six feet of snake were attained at the expense of my chickens. . . .'

At this point Mr Castro's car drew up in front of our house. Papa walked up to him, and Mama went to talk to Sartina. I followed after Papa.

'Good afternoon, Mr Castro. . . .'

'Listen, Tchembene, I've just found out that my pointer is dead, and his chest's all swollen. My natives tell me that he came howling from your house before he died. I don't want any back-chat, and I'm just telling you – either you pay compensation or I'll make a complaint at the Administration. He was the best pointer I ever had.'

'I've just come back from work – I don't know anything . . .'

'I don't care a damn about that. Don't argue. Are you going to pay or aren't you?'

'But, Mr Castro . . .'

'Mr Castro nothing. It's eight pounds. And it's better if the matter rests here.'

'As you like, Mr Castro, but I don't have the money now. . . .'

'We'll see about that later. I'll wait until the end of the month, and if you don't pay then there'll be a row.'

'Mr Castro, we've known each other such a long time, and there's never . . .'

'Don't try that with me. I know what you all need – a bloody good hiding is the only thing. . . .'

Mr Castro climbed into his car and pulled away. Papa stayed watching while the car drove off. 'Son of a bitch. . . .'

I went up to him, and tugged at the sleeve of his coat.

'Papa, why didn't you say that to his face?'

He didn't answer.

We had hardly finished supper when Papa said, 'Mother,

E

tell Sartina to clear the table quickly. My children, let us pray. Today we are not going to read the Bible. We will simply pray.'

Papa talked in Ronga, and for this reason I regretted having asked him that question a while ago.

When Sartina finished clearing away the plates and folded the cloth, Papa began, 'Tatana, ha ku dumba hosi ya tilo ni misaba . . .'

When he finished, his eyes were red.

Amen!

Amen!

Mama got up, and asked, as if it meant nothing, 'But what did Mr Castro want, after all?'

'It's nothing important.'

'All right, tell me about it in our room. I'll go and set out the children's things. You, Ginho, wake up early tomorrow and take a laxative. . . .'

When they had all gone away, I asked Papa, 'Papa, why do you always pray when you are very angry?'

'Because He is the best counsellor.'

'And what counsel does He give you?'

'He gives me no counsel. He gives me strength to continue.'

'Papa, do you believe a lot in Him?'

Papa looked at me as if he were seeing me for the first time, and then exploded, 'My son, one must have a hope. When one comes to the end of a day, and one knows that tomorrow will be another day just like it, and that things will always be the same, we have got to find the strength to keep on smiling, and keep on saying, "This is not important!" We ourselves have to allot our own reward for all the heroism of every day. We have to establish a date for this reward, even if it's the day of our death! Even today you saw Mr Castro humiliate me: this formed only part of today's portion, because there were many things that happened that you didn't see. No, my son, there must be a hope! It must exist! Even if all this only denies Him, He must exist!'

Papa stopped suddenly, and forced himself to smile. Then he added, 'Even a poor man has to have something. Even if it is only a hope! Even if it's a false hope!'

'Papa, I could have prevented the snake from biting Mr Castro's dog. . . .'

Papa looked at me with his eyes full of tenderness, and said under his breath, 'It doesn't matter. It's a good thing that he got bitten.'

Mama appeared at the door. 'Are you going to let the child go to sleep or not?'

I looked at Papa, and we remembered Mr Castro and both of us burst out laughing. Mama didn't understand.

'Are you two going crazy?'

'Yes, and it's about time we went crazy,' said Papa with a smile.

Papa was already on the way to his room, but I must have talked too loudly. Anyway, it was better that he heard, 'Papa, I sometimes . . . I don't really know . . . but for some time . . . I have been thinking that I didn't love you all. I'm sorry. . . .'

Mama didn't understand what we had been saying, so she became angry. 'Stop all this, or else . . .'

'Do you know, my son,' Papa spoke ponderously, and gesticulated a lot before every word. 'The most difficult thing to bear is that feeling of complete emptiness . . . and one suffers very much . . . very, very, very much. One grows with so much bottled up inside, but afterwards it is difficult to scream, you know.'

'Papa, and when Mr Castro comes? . . .'

Mama was going to object, but Papa clutched her shoulder firmly. 'It's nothing, Mother, but, you know, our son believes that people don't mount wild horses, and that they only make use of the hungry, docile ones. Yet when a horse goes wild it gets shot down, and it's all finished.

But tame horses die every day. Every day, d'you hear?
Day after day after day – as long as they can stand on
their feet.'

Mama looked at him with her eyes popping out.

'Do you know, Mother, I'm afraid to believe that this is
true, but I also can't bring myself to tell him that it's a
lie . . . He sees, even today he saw . . . I only wish for the
strength to make sure that my children know how to
recognize other things. . . .'

Papa and Mama were already in their room, so I
couldn't hear any more, but even from there Mama
yelled, 'Tomorrow you'll take a laxative, that'll show you.
I'm not like your father who lets himself get taken in. . . .'

My bed was flooded in yellow moonlight, and it was
pleasant to feel my naked skin quiver with its cold caress.
For some unknown reason the warm sensation of Sartina's
body flowed through my senses. I managed to cling to her
almost physical presence for a few minutes, and I wanted
to fall asleep with her so as not to dream of dogs and
snakes.

NOTES

Capulana : colourful cloth worn as a garment, sarong style

Ronga : the language spoken by the Ronga people who live in
the area around Lourenço Marques

Nhoka : snake

Tatana, ha ku dumba hosi ya tilo ni misaba: 'Father, we put our trust
in Thee, Lord of heaven and earth'

JACK COPE

JACK COPE, a farmer's son, poet, short-story writer, novelist, was born on a farm in Natal in 1913. He started work as a newspaper man, but soon dropped journalism. He worked in England for four years before the Second World War, then returned to farming in Natal. He has published two books of verse and an historical biography as well as plays and novels. His first novel, *The Fair House*, was published in London in 1955, and since then it has gone into many editions and translations. *The Golden Oriole* followed in 1958, *The Road to Ysterberg* in 1959 and a fourth, *Albino*, was published in London this year. He founded *Contrast*, the South African literary magazine, in 1960. At present he is working on a new novel, *Motaung*.

This short story, taken from Jack Cope's collection, *The Tame Ox*, is played out in a shanty town high up above Cape Town. In it we meet Benjamin Segode, frustrated and bitter, the Secretary of the Vigilance Society, who vents his spleen on a young white missionary girl sent to teach Christianity to the local inhabitants because the white priest is too busy with his own white congregation.

The Little Missionary

He came out of the shadow of the bush path and blinked in the sun. The clearing was scattered with refuse and tufts of dry marsh-grass struggling to keep a foothold against the bush. The sun beat on his head but he was listening and took no notice of the heat and of the flies that buzzed up at any slight movement. His face hardened and he ran his tongue quickly over his full, strong lips. He could hear them singing, children singing a hymn tune on a Sunday morning. Which direction did the voices come from?

The willow bush stretched on for miles, criss-crossed by a thousand paths. One minute you were hidden in the dense acrid-smelling foliage, your footsteps muffled in soft white sand; the next, you were in the midst of a shanty cluster. Thousands of shanties and pondokkies grew over-night with the swiftness of a malignant fungus in the bush. They were the homes of the people flocking like migrant birds, with an urgent necessity, to the city. Once the land had been gleaming white dunes, until the willow bush crept over it and bound down the moving sand and shut out the sea-haze and the great blue outline of Table Mountain in sky-space above the city. Now the shanty-clusters brought a half-wild life into the bush. The axe was heard; women laughed and hens clucked; men shouted to one another over the tree-tops.

He remembered how the police sometimes came; they tramped along the maze of sandpaths at night carrying flashlights, keeping together in parties of a hundred or more with reinforcements waiting beside the nearest roads. Next day the shanty-dwellers would set their life in order again, talking with a low hum of voices, cursing. Some-times a song would start, a song of lamenting, and among those who joined in would be a few with tear-brimmed eyes.

On that Sunday morning Benjamin Segode listened to a different kind of a song, a Christmas hymn of rejoicing. He had been brought up a Christian at a Mission in Basutoland. His father was a churchwarden and people said there was no one for a week's journey who could preach like him. Benjamin had saddened his father, asking why he, the best preacher in Mafeteng, swept the church floor while the white missionary was up in the pulpit and could hardly make himself understood. His father had said: 'God's will is not always plain for a boy to see.' Benjamin had left Basutoland and had never returned. Though he remembered his father's sorrowing voice and resigned expression of face and hands, he had not stopped asking questions. His Sesotho Bible lay, carefully wrapped, in the bottom of his tin box and he felt its presence there like his father's voice, reproachful, full of distant music.

He wiped his face with a red handkerchief before he pushed aside the foliage and went on. He walked slowly, picked a leaf involuntarily and bit it, tasting the sharp, astringent juice. The veins pulsed in his neck and anger was rising in his wide, upward-slanting eyes. He had a mouth turned up at the corners too, so that in his utmost temper there would still remain the shadowy semblance of a smile.

The singing came to him more distinctly as he pushed on with muffled steps along the path. Children's voices, not in his language but in Afrikaans, the language of the white man. That was what he disliked and suspected.

Then he was out in a big clearing. Six or seven dwellings sprawled among a few tall trees. Close by was the pon-dokkie of a woodhawker opening on a sandy yard where he kept his two donkeys, stacks of cut wood, chopping-blocks and everywhere untidy heaps of wood chips, bark, refuse. The donkeys stood in the sun on three legs, leaning their necks over the fence. The woodhawker himself was slouched asleep against his pondokkie wall while his wife stooped over a washing tub full of soapsuds. Neither took any notice of the singers. Benjamin Segode looked at them carefully and counted the children – twenty or more of them sitting and standing in a little circle under the shade of a large willow. The tree grew at the far corner of the woodhawker's yard and trailed its ragged branches over two more shanties standing back to back on the other side of the fence. The singing was led by a pretty white girl of fourteen or fifteen. She stood with her back to the tree, Bible in hand, and sunlight filtering through the leaves made bright moving dots on her white cotton dress and her blonde hair braided in two plaits over her shoulders.

Benjamin stood at the edge of the bush. None of them had seen him.

'O die vrolike, o die salige,
    Vredebringende Kersfeestyd . . .'

– the child voices sang with a lift –

'O joyful and blessed, peace-bringing Christmastide . . .
    Holy choirs of angels sing the happy news . . .'

He walked out towards the woman at the wash-tub until his shadow fell across the soapsuds and she looked up quickly.

'Dumela,' he said quietly.

'Dumela, Segode,' she greeted him, smiling. Then she caught the look in his eye and glanced across, suddenly scared, to where her husband dozed in the sun.

'Is there trouble?' she asked in a low voice.

'You should know.' His gaze turned to the girl and her Sunday school.

She did not follow his meaning. 'Here is Benjamin Segode,' she sang out to her husband. The sleeping man stirred and settled back, his hat pushed still farther over his face.

'Are your children there too?' Benjamin jerked his head towards the big tree. She was a little alarmed by the question and stood with the soapy water falling in drops off her fingers. Then she nodded. 'My children and the other children.'

She stood with her back to the tree, Bible in hand

'How can you sell them – are they cattle?'

'I do not sell my own children. Segode, what are you saying?'

She dried her hands on her apron, looking away from him, and walked with heavy steps to the pondokkie. 'Wake up.' She touched her husband on the shoulder. 'Here is a visitor.'

The wood-seller sat up and yawned.

'Ho, Segode!' he held out a hand genially. 'Dumela, brother.'

'Dumela.'

'What brings us the good luck of this visit, Mr Secretary?'

Benjamin warmed to the man's good-natured manner. He would have liked to squat at his side and smoke a cigarette with him there in the sun. But he stood back unbending.

'Do your eyes see what mine do?' he asked.

'Brother, I think they do.'

'That?' And he pointed expressively with his middle finger at the circle of children and the white girl at the far end of the yard beyond the donkeys.

The wood-seller stood up. 'Is there anything against that?' He screwed up the corners of his eyes.

'You must answer for yourself,' Benjamin said, feeling the heat and indignation rising up again in his veins. The woman had gone round to the other side of the pondokkie and he could hear her voice in a soft cooing tone call to someone out of sight. 'Ah, here is our Vigilance secretary, Benjamin Segode.' Voices answered from the bush, quietly, like the note of the Cape robin.

'It keeps the children out of mischief and no harm is done,' the woodhawker said in a conciliating manner.

'You gave her permission to teach in your yard?'

The man nodded and tried to smile although he could see the secretary had brought a flame of anger to singe him.

'No – you cut wood all day,' Benjamin said, 'and you have a heart of wood and a brain of wood. Are you all the same – does your wife have soapy water in her veins? No harm is done! You hand over to them the children of our people; you, Washington Mahleke, sell your own flesh and blood for a morning on your back in the sun!'

'Hai, Segode!' the wood-seller cut in.

'Why can't you keep them out of mischief yourselves? Teach them to be true men and girls, teach them the songs of our race that are forgotten here in this stinking marsh. Teach them to rise up out of the mud.'

The wood-seller tugged his beard nervously. The secretary was a younger man than he and, by rights, had no business to give him such a rating. But he drew a deep breath and said bitterly: 'There is some truth in what you say, Segode.'

Benjamin waited in silence until their eyes met. He hated the indolence of people who could forget everything in a song or could dance the moon down into the gleaming ocean, dreaming of a full life, and of friendship and peace until the sun woke them up in the naked helplessness of their poverty. He saw his words had shaken Washington Mahleke and touched a hidden sore. Again he mopped his face with the red handkerchief and walked over to the Sunday-school circle. The dry twigs cracked under his boots. The children looked round to see who came, gladly letting their attention wander from the lesson. They had stopped singing and the white girl was reading to them from the Bible. Most of them were pure blacks but there were a few Cape coloured children among them and all could understand the language they spoke, which was Afrikaans. The girl was reading in Afrikaans and held open her Bible in both hands. A ray of sunshine shone through the stray wisps of her blonde hair on the pages of the Book. She paused, looking at Benjamin Segode with her bright greenish eyes.

'Go on,' he said.

She was reading from Genesis the story of the dis-inheriting of Ishmael, son of the Egyptian bondwoman.

'"And Sarah saw the son of Hagar the Egyptian, which she had born unto Abraham, mocking."'

She looked up from the page and noticed the sinister smile of the black man.

'Go on,' Segode repeated.

'"Wherefore she said to Abraham: Cast out this bond-woman and her son, for the son of this bond-woman shall not be heir with my son, even with Isaac."'

The girl's lips quivered and she could not read farther. Benjamin Segode stepped between the sitting children and approached her. She had turned paler and watched him with a fixed look. He could see now she had brown flecks in the green of her eyes. They were firm, steady eyes, wide open and glistening. Involuntarily she had pressed the open Book against her bosom and waited, standing her ground.

'Good morning – and who sent you here to do this?' he said in English.

'I'm sorry, I don't speak that language.'

He repeated his words in Afrikaans with the thick over-tone of a Basuto accent. He knew five languages and the babel of the new slums was easy to him. The girl frowned in the effort to decide whether she could answer a black man's questions. Then she said honestly: 'The Dominie sent me!'

'What is your name?'

'Angelina du Preez.'

'So the Dominie sends you and you come here alone to preach to the heathens. Why doesn't he come himself?'

'He is too busy – he has to preach to the white people at three services and baptize and teach the Catechism.'

'He's not afraid to come here?'

She flushed. 'No, he is not afraid.'

'He marks the Book for you and the chapters you must read and the hymns to sing?'

'Yes.'

'And you believe in God and Jesus Christ and the Saints?'

She frowned again and decided not to answer. The strange, flickering smile of the man was beginning to freeze her. Black people were coming from all sides as if there were no reason for coming but simply a chance they happened along that way. Men with a jacket hung on one shoulder, a woman hitching up a baby in the blanket on her back, older children with long bare legs and bare feet shuffling in a half-dance through the sand. They all stopped in different groups when they were some way off and seemed to be speaking to one another, yet she felt they were watching her, listening to her every word. She was a long way, more than a mile, more than half an hour's walk through the bush on heavy sand-paths to the nearest white man's house. She could scream and her voice would be lost in the willows.

'Does the Dominie also give you sweets for the children?' Benjamin asked her.

'No.' Her face clouded with bitter resentment at the unjust question. 'I buy sweets for them out of my own pocket money.'

He turned to the children. 'Do you like sweets on a Sunday morning?'

They did not answer but lowered their big wondering eyes to avoid his sneering look. They loved their little teacher and were troubled and a little panic-stricken at the manner and tone of the powerful secretary.

'Let me see your Book?' He waited to receive it. But she was suspicious and pressed it still tighter to her as if to protect it with her life.

'Why are you afraid to let me see it – is it not a good Book?'

'Yes, it's the one and only Book.'

Slowly and reluctantly she yielded up the Bible and he took it in both hands with the traditional African courtesy. To take anything with one hand was an affront to the giver. He saw it was marked in a number of places with small pieces of black ribbon, but he did not trouble to see what the Dutch Reformed minister had set for reading. It was easy to find in the great Book he had been brought up on a justification, or at least a point of argument, for almost anything – for peace as well as for violence and treachery, for avarice and deceit and hatred, or for love and goodness. He knew how oppression could be sanctified as the curse of God on Ham or the casting out of the sons of Ishmael and the choosing of Israel. It was not honest, it was not the spirit of the Book; but it was done. Benjamin closed the pages and held it flat between the palms of his hands. It was a finely printed Bible bound in black American cloth with the paper edges tinted red.

'Juffrou du Preez, we black people know this book – do you understand? We have had it for more than a hundred years, two hundred. It is full of good, it is written in a way that the heart of a man understands. But I say we should put it away for a time. I mean that we do not accept it from you. Do you hear? We do not believe you, we do not trust you – you little girl, and your Dominies and your rich men and your soldiers and policemen. When we are equal and free we will take up the Bible again. Then we will be happy with it and no one will make us afraid. Is that understood?'

He raised his voice and she pressed her back against the tree with a sense of terror, watching him, and beyond him the hundreds of black people gradually closing up.

'Is it understood?' he demanded again.

'I don't understand. I have done nothing wrong.'

'No, Juffrou du Preez' – he gave a short deep laugh –

'you have done right, by your own people. You have come here to capture our children as slaves.'

'Aah, that is a terrible thing to say. It is not true, I vow and swear it is not true.'

'Well we have had enough. But your Dominie sends you to preach your laws.'

'I have preached no laws.'

'You think you are above us and can talk down to our children because your white Parliament has passed a hundred Acts to lower us.'

'That is politics, and I know nothing about it. I have never heard of such Acts or talked about them. If you say false things before these children, then I deny them and God is my only witness of the truth.'

She was white-faced and the pink had drained even out of her lips. But she spoke back at him with a desperate courage, putting him into a rage.

'The truth, the truth,' he shouted contemptuously. 'Every lie is the truth for your kind. You twist everything to suit yourselves.'

Somebody laughed in the crowd behind him, and from the menace in that laugh she felt her knees grow soft and tremble.

Benjamin Segode handed back the Bible.

'Nou vat jou Boek en trek' (take your Bible and clear out), he said in a controlled voice. She stood a moment pressing it to her thudding heart.

'Trek, trek!' he shouted.

And, without knowing what she was doing, she began to run. A little figure in white in the gleaming sunlight, her blonde hair-braids tied with white ribbons flying out behind her and the Bible, black and red, clutched under one arm. The people in the woodhawker's yard parted to let her go. She ran past the iron wash-tub swimming with soap-suds and past the woodhawker himself at his door with a slender home-made pipe between his teeth.

In a few seconds she was out of the yard and had plunged down one of the sandy paths into the tunnel of the bush. There she saw a single black man coming her way, and in her panic she ran on straight towards him, almost into his arms. Surprised, he stepped aside, pushing into the wall of leaves to let her pass. Her feet sank deep into the sand at each step, and running was like the cloying horror of a nightmare.

Angelina du Preez did not know how long or how far she ran when she came to a stop. There was a taste of blood in her throat and her heart was knocking and jolting as if it would leap out of her breast. It was the first time she had ever felt like that. Her legs were weak and heavy almost as though detached from her body. At first she listened for anyone who might be following her. There was no sound except the faint crackle of the bush seeds ripening in the sun and the swish of the leaves stirred by a slight eddy. That was all she could hear for a while, holding her breath; that, and the drumming in her ears. Somewhere a cock crowed; far off, out of sight, an aeroplane hummed in the sky. She longed just to catch sight of it, but the strip of sky above the path was narrow and gave her no view. She could not tell where she was or which way she should now go to get back on the tarmac road, the cars passing and the houses of white people. She changed her Bible into the other hand, thinking what to do.

Trying to fix her bearings, she was certain of one thing alone – the direction from which she had run. Should she continue and trust to chance? But doing so, she might stumble upon more bunches of unknown hostile pondokkies, she might encounter a skolly gangster drunk and treacherous on the lonely bush path. It was cowardly to hold such fears, and she tried to fight them down in her mind. 'God help me, Lord God help me,' she prayed.

In that vague, rustling emptiness with every bush watching her and maybe concealing something, she had nothing to grip on to, nothing but the thought of the little children she had come to teach and to know. Sunday after Sunday she had found them waiting for her. Surely they had grown to love her in their own way and no harm would come to her among them. It had been a foolish and mad thing to run away from the native leader, for she had thus accepted his charge of wrong, of untruth and twisting. And in one minute of fear she had lost the children and undone the work and the first mission of her young life. How could she explain it? If she were to set right her mistake she must go back and face the black people, whatever the consequences, whatever the danger and threat to her life itself. There was no other way. 'O Lord God help me,' she prayed.

The way back was plain to find. She simply turned and followed the path, going neither to right nor left. But at each step, at each sound from the bush, her courage sagged. Then, after what seemed a long time, she heard a murmur of human voices somewhere ahead, and she had to stop to let her heart slow down. The voices became louder as she continued.

At last she reached the edge of the clearing near the wood-seller's fenced-in yard and peered out from among the foliage. Where she had taken her Sunday school class, under the same sheltering tree, the secretary was holding a meeting. He spoke slowly and expressively in a language she did not understand and hundreds of people in the yard responded to him with rumbling voices or with a sigh. They had their backs to her. The native leader had turned her cowardly running away into a success for himself. On the edge of the crowd were the children, her children. They were not listening, but seemed drawn by the stir and passion among their elders.

She walked out across the sand into the full sunlight.

They noticed her at once. A murmur came from them and hundreds of dark faces turned towards her. The secretary stopped in the middle of his speech. Some of the children started talking excitedly, but their elders hushed them.

She came near the children and opened her mouth, but her throat was dry and no sound emerged. Again she tried and said huskily: 'Children, I have one more thing to say and one hymn to sing with you before I go today. . . .'

She did not know how to continue, and there was a silence.

Then she said: 'Will you listen to me, my children?'

A small boy hiding behind a companion piped up 'No!' A faint rustle like a deep breath rose from the crowd.

'Gracie, will you listen to me?' Angelina appealed.

A little black girl with her crimpy hair done in a dozen plaits said softly : 'Ja, my nonnatjie.'

'No!' shouted another shrill voice.

Then one of the children picked up a wood chip and tossed it at the white girl. It grazed her sunburnt leg and left a slight scratch and a bead of blood. Another chip followed and another, until in a moment they were all pelting her as hard as they could, laughing and jeering at her. Some chips hit her and some flew past. They did not hurt her; she could not feel them. But the wound they made was deep in her breast.

She stood there in the sunlight and bowed her head and began to cry.

Benjamin Segode rushed from his place at the tree and stopped the children throwing wood chips. 'Hai!' he hissed at them furiously. 'What is this – are you hooligans?'

The children shrank back among the people and the whole crowd fell quite silent. Some watched and some turned away their eyes while the white girl stood there and cried, shaken with long choking sobs, and the tears ran down her small face and dropped in the hot sand.

NOTES

pondokkies : shanties, makeshift houses composed of cardboard
   and zinc sheets
dumela : greetings
'*Ja, my nonnatjie*' : 'Yes, my little madam.'

OTHER BOOKS BY JACK COPE

The Fair House (MacGibbon & Kee, 1955)
The Golden Oriole (Heinemann, 1958)
The Road to Ysterberg (Heinemann, 1959)
Albino (Heinemann, 1964).

CYPRIAN EKWENSI

CYPRIAN EKWENSI was born in Northern Nigeria but belongs to the Ibo tribe of Eastern Nigeria. He was educated at Government College, Ibadan and later trained as a pharmacist in England. He is a former head of the Features Department of the Nigerian Broadcasting Corporation, and is now Director of Information Services of the Federation of Nigeria. His novel, *People of the City*, was the first novel by a Nigerian to be published on a world-wide scale.

Burning Grass is a tale of Northern Nigeria, and tells of the Fulani cattlemen who move southwards towards the banks of the Niger. Mai Sunsaye, the chief of Dokan Toro, is bewitched and chases after the Sokugo, a bird which strikes without warning and induces the wandering sickness. He continues through many experiences and adventures until he is finally reunited with his family and cured by the herbs of the ex-slave Fatimeh.

This excerpt tells how he is first lured away by the bird, and how his huts are fired, his cattle stolen and his family dispersed by his rival Ardo.

The Sokugo

Mai Sunsaye sat outside the hut, reading under the dorowa tree. He was much versed in the Koran, and he read and wrote Arabic with a fluency not unusual among high priests of the wandering Fulani. He made charms and amulets, he doctored the sick, he was a sage highly respected in the village of Dokan Toro. From far and near, his clients brought him their wounds of body and of soul.

As he pored over his books his neck ached. He was an old man, but he seldom spared himself or even remembered that tiredness came easily these days. He lifted his head so as to ease the muscles of his neck. It was a simple act, such as a man might unconsciously perform a hundred times a day. But for Mai Sunsaye it was a decisive act.

In that particular interval of time, his eyes fell on a dove. It was nothing, really, just a Senegal dove, grey-breasted and red-toed against the sun-dried leaves. Mai Sunsaye saw hundreds of Senegal doves every day because he lived in their natural habitat, the sparsely wooded thorn scrub. That day he had seen oh, he had never really tried to count them. They were always there; mating, eating the grain, cooing in the woody patches that dotted the endless veld.

'Kuku-roo-ku-doo! . . . kuku-roo-ku-doo! . . .'

He tiptoed across the clearing among the dung, with the fowls scattering to left and right of him. The dove had seen him. It had stopped cooing. It looked suspiciously down, golden eyes rolling. A quick flutter and it began to climb from branch to branch, skipping lightly. A talisman – a small rectangular fold of parchment – was clearly visible to Sunsaye. It trailed after the dove as it skipped.

With his weak eyes he followed the bird's movements, straining hard against the glare of the sun. And then he saw it leap out of the tree and flash away, sweeping over the shimmering grassland and describing huge exciting arcs. He was barely able to see it drop into a tree. His robe caught against the thorn scrub, and every now and again he paused to adjust the sandals and to ease his feet.

If only Mai Sunsaye had at that moment remembered

the sokugo, that charm of the Fulani cattlemen, a magic
that turned studious men into wanderers, that led husbands
to desert their wives, Chiefs their people and sane men
their reason, Sunsaye would have refused to pursue the
dove any farther. Instead, all he could feel now was an
exhilaration of the spirit that gave a strange buoyancy to
his whole bearing. He felt he could easily grow wings and
overtake the dove.

The dove had alighted in a low gardenia with twisted
branches. He fixed his eyes on that tree, and as he
approached he heard it cooing again. He broke through
the thorn thicket, scurrying the bush rats, frightening the
duiker into the blazing sun. He cursed as a black mass
uncoiled itself and slid swiftly under the grass. A cobra!

'Kuku-roo-ku-doo! . . .' came the sweet, enticing notes.
He saw the flutter of wings, the climbing out of the tree
in little hops, until, at the topmost branch, the dove took
off. He swore. He shaded his eyes and admired the graceful
agility of the dove. The bird swept big arcs in the sky,
made sudden deceptive dives as though intending to
alight, spread its tail fanwise to act as a brake; and suddenly it froze and seemed to drop into a date palm. Sunsaye knew a short cut to that date palm. Turn back now!
He seemed to hear the words from somewhere inside him.

But he went forward, not stopping to question, and
followed the dove with the talisman as it lured him on
and on; farther and farther into the grassland and the
thorn trees and acacia gum. On he went till the sun sank
lower and lower and dipped below the horizon and dusk
came, and he was hungry and thirsty.

In the thorn forest, in the very heart of rock and stream,
darkness could mean encounter with the agents of swift
death: the big wild cows, the leopard. But Mai Sunsaye
was beyond caring.

Mai Sunsaye's wife, Shaitu, had been out to sell sour

milk in the neighbouring town. When she stooped to enter the next little hut where Mai Sunsaye often sat, her copper ear-rings dangled. She did not let it cross her mind that he could be anywhere else but within the settlement or that if he was not he would be far away.

Her daughter Liebe lay sleeping on a mat. She shook her. Liebe awoke and told a story of three strange men she had seen that afternoon. She said that the men came with a cage full of birds and let out one dove with a talisman attached to its foot. She led her mother to the back of the hut and showed her where Mai Sunsaye had been reading. Flung about in some haste was a book, a slate, an over-turned inkpot – all Mai Sunsaye's.

Shaitu looked about her for a clue.

'There were three men,' Leibe said. 'One was a Chief.'

'How d'you know?'

'Mother, he wore a crest on his turban.'

'They must be evil men; I suspect it is your father's rival, Ardo and his people. Since the people chose your father as Chief, Ardo has never been happy. He has sought to do away with him by malicious gossip. And now he has brought on him the sokugo.'

Shaitu's life, like that of any other cattle Fulani, was ruled by beliefs for which she could find no logical explanation. She accepted happenings but associated them with inanimate objects and peculiar circumstances. A talisman could bring luck. . . . A man may strike his enemy down by calling his name aloud and firing a needle into the sky. A man could send his enemy wandering to his death by striking him with the sokugo, the wandering charm. This was what she concluded had been done to her husband. Her belief in omens and portents was steadfast, and Liebe's description tallied with the manner of the black magicians among the cattle Fulani. Liebe told how Ardo men let out a dove with a talisman tied to its foot, how the dove flew into a tree with Sunsaye following after it. She was only a little girl and Shaitu, hearing the detail she gave, knew she was telling what she had seen.

'They have struck him,' she concluded. 'It is the sokugo.'

It could only be the sokugo, the wandering disease. Now she knew he would wander after anything on the wing, until someone destroyed Ardo's magic. Thus did the sokugo deprive men of their stable lives and send them stupidly wandering.

How to punish Ardo? When Rikku returned from the grazing fields they must think of a way.

Shaitu waited and waited. It seemed to her that Rikku would never come home. At last she saw him in the valley among the cattle lumbering slowly towards the camp. She did not return his smile, but helped him tie up the cattle for the night and light the big smudge-fire that kept away the leopards and the hyenas. When they had finished, Rikku asked casually, 'Where's father?'

'I haven't seen him,' Shaitu said carelessly. 'But I don't think he's gone far.'

'He seldom goes out!'

'I don't know, Rikku. I returned and did not meet him.' She gave him a bowl of gruel. 'Drink this, my son, and don't worry. You must be tired after grazing the cattle all day in the sun.'

Rikku found a log and sat on it.

'I can guess where he's gone,' he said. 'He's gone to see what the medicine-man will do about my love-sickness.' He laughed.

'Perhaps so, my son.'

Liebe came from the hut and said, 'Mother, won't you tell him about the three men I saw?'

'You saw three men?' Rikku put aside the bowl.

'Yes. They carried cages, and – and – birds!'

'Liebe!' said Shaitu sharply. 'Go back and pound the

corn.' She turned to Rikku. 'Do not mind your younger sister. She's only talking.'

'But who were they?'

'Strangers. Bird-catchers, I think.'

'And my father went with them?'

'Rikku, your questions are too many! Finish now and have your rest while I make supper. Is it not enough that your father is out and will soon be back?'

Shaitu went on with her husking and Rikku with his meal in silence. He went inside the hut to take off his leather apron. She dared not let Rikku know what she secretly believed, that the sokugo was at work on his father. If Rikku believed that his father had gone to bring back the girl he loved, it was much better not to undeceive him.

Rikku woke in the small hours of the morning. Something, a slight unusualness in the air, had awakened him. He sat up with that immediate instinct of the nomad, developed over a lifetime of exposure to danger from man, beast and nature. It seemed to him that the cattle were milling around uneasily. He listened. No dogs were barking. But why? Had a spell been cast over them? He felt the restlessness spreading among the cattle. He heard real commotion now, as if someone was trying to stampede the bulls.

'Rikku!' Shaitu shouted from somewhere in the dark.

'Mother! Thieves . . . Get up. Thieves!'

A burst of uncontrolled movement shattered the night. Rikku slid under the door of the hut and out into the night. He saw a group of men – mere shapes – emerge from the darkness. The turbaned one was whispering commands, pointing. The other two in leather bags moved with precision, their daggers gleaming. They were cutting the cattle loose. From behind a pile of logs, Rikku watched them, crouching. Cattle stumbled blindly past him and crashed into the huts, whipped to recklessness by the shrieking orders of the men behind them. Rikku leapt aside, dodging a sharp object thrust at his ribs from behind. In an instant they had bound his hands behind his back, and made off. He heard his mother and the children screaming from the other hut, felt the choking smell of the burning thatch followed by the sharp crackle of uncertain flames, then the whole settlement burst into one blinding sheet of flame, frightful to behold. His father's huts caught one spark; his mother's hut seemed to reach out a hand and to catch another flying spark. The sparks glowed in the wind, and soon those huts crackled alight.

'Liebe! Liebe!' Shaitu cried. 'Rikku! Don't let Liebe burn to death.'

'They have tied my hands!' Rikku yelled.

He saw the dark figures busy with the sinister work; flitting in and out of the cattle, cutting them loose, hurrying them away. Then in one final upward surge that dazzled the eyes, Rikku saw in the flaming mass the last indelible picture of his father's camp burning to ashes. He would never, as long as he lived, forget the choking smoke fumes drifting across the thorn, the upturned hoofs of the stampeding cattle, the red heart of the glowing fire that had once been a hut. He realized that the enemy had once again out-generalled him, and his heart sank. What remained deeply impressed in his memory was that face: a glimpse of it, dark, with a golden crest on the turban, catching the playing flames with now a dazzle, now a dull glow, and the tightly set teeth from which the commands issued.

The man was Ardo. Rikku knew of him; he had heard his father describe Ardo as his greatest rival for the chieftaincy of Dokan Toro. This man, Rikku remembered, had been seen in the afternoon by Liebe, releasing the dove with the talisman attached to its foot.

Did he aim to exterminate the entire family? If so, it must be true what Liebe had said that his father had been struck with the wandering disease and had not gone in quest of Fatimeh as Rikku had imagined, but was merely wandering aimlessly over the veld. He must be pursued and saved.

Rikku worked his wrists, hoping to break the knots. But Ardo's men had done their work well.

OTHER BOOKS BY CYPRIAN EKWENSI

People of the City (Andrew Dakers, 1954; Heinemann Educational Books, 1963)

The Passport of Mallam Ilia (C.U.P., 1960)

The Drummer Boy (C.U.P., 1960)

Burning Grass (Heinemann, 1962)

Jagua Nana (Hutchinson, 1961)

An African Night's Entertainment (African Universities Press, 1962)

Beautiful Feathers (Hutchinson, 1963)

AMOS TUTUOLA

AMOS TUTUOLA was born in 1920 at Abeokuta, Nigeria. He received a primary school education at the local Central School, and then was forced to abandon his education at the death of his father. He was firstly employed as a blacksmith and then by the Department of Labour, Lagos, to take finger-prints. He has at present five novels to his credit.

The Palm Wine Drinkard was the first West African novel to make any impact on the English reading public. This is more a prose epic, a fantasy set in the world of living and dead, where everything is possible. The basis of the novel is the quest of the Drinkard, who calls himself 'Father of the Gods who can do everything in this world', for his dead tapster. After many strange and fascinating adventures he is finally forced to return home without the tapster, and then rids his townsfolk of famine by appeasing the wrath of the Male Sky God. This excerpt shows how the Drinkard rescues the beautiful daughter of the head of one of the towns he passes through, a woman he later marries, from The Curious Creature, the Complete Gentleman. The language usage is peculiar to Tutuola and is not limited by correct syntax or grammatical function.

The Complete Gentleman

THE DESCRIPTION OF THE CURIOUS CREATURE

He was a beautiful 'complete' gentleman, he dressed with the finest and most costly clothes, all the parts of his body were completed, he was a tall man but stout. As this gentleman came to the market on that day, if he had been an article or animal for sale, he would be sold at least for £2,000 (two thousand pounds). As this complete gentleman came to the market on that day, and at the same time that this lady saw him in the market, she did nothing more than to ask him where he was living, but this fine gentleman did not answer her or approach her at all. But when she noticed that the fine or complete gentleman did not listen to her, she left her articles and began to watch the movements of the complete gentleman about in the market and left her articles unsold.

By and by the market closed for that day then the whole people in the market were returning to their destinations, etc., and the complete gentleman was returning to his own too, but as this lady was following him about in the market all the while, she saw him when he was returning to his destination as others did, then she was following him (complete gentleman) to an unknown place. But as she was following the complete gentleman along the road, he was telling her to go back and not to follow him, but the lady did not listen to what he was telling her, and when the complete gentleman had tired of telling her not to follow him or to go back to her town, he left her to follow him.

'DO NOT FOLLOW UNKNOWN
MAN'S BEAUTY'

But when they had travelled about twelve miles away
from that market, they left the road on which they were
travelling and started to travel inside an endless forest
in which only all the terrible creatures were living.

'RETURN THE PARTS OF BODY TO THE OWNERS; OR HIRED PARTS OF THE COMPLETE GENTLEMAN'S BODY TO BE RETURNED'

As they were travelling along in this endless forest then
the complete gentleman in the market that the lady was
following, began to return the hired parts of his body to
the owners and he was paying them the rentage money.
When he reached where he hired the left foot, he pulled
it out, he gave it to the owner and paid him, and they
kept going; when they reached the place where he hired
the right foot, he pulled it out and gave it to the owner
and paid for the rentage. Now both feet had returned to
the owners, so he began to crawl along on the ground,
by that time, that lady wanted to go back to her town or
her father, but the terrible and curious creature or the
complete gentleman did not allow her to return or go
back to her town or her father again and the complete
gentleman said thus:

'I had told you not to follow me before we branched
into this endless forest which belongs to only terrible and
curious creatures, but when I became a half-bodied
incomplete gentleman you wanted to go back, now that
cannot be done, you have failed. Even you have never
seen anything yet, just follow me.'

When they went furthermore, then they reached where
he hired the belly, ribs, chest, etc., then he pulled them
out and gave them to the owner and paid for the rentage.

Now to this gentleman or terrible creature remained
only the head and both arms with neck, by that time he
could not crawl as before but only went jumping on as a
bull-frog and now this lady was soon faint for this fearful

Now both feet had returned to the owners, so he began to crawl on the ground

creature whom she was following. But when the lady saw
every part of this complete gentleman in the market was
spared or hired and he was returning them to the owners,
then she began to try all her efforts to return to her father's
town, but she was not allowed by this fearful creature
at all.

When they reached where he hired both arms, he
pulled them out and gave them to the owner, he paid
for them; and they were still going on in this endless
forest, they reached the place where he hired the neck, he
pulled it out and gave it to the owner and paid for it as
well.

'A FULL-BODIED GENTLEMAN
REDUCED TO HEAD'

Now this complete gentleman was reduced to head and
when they reached where he hired the skin and flesh
which covered the head, he returned them, and
paid to the owner, now the complete gentleman in the
market reduced to a 'SKULL' and this lady remained with
only 'Skull'. When the lady saw that she remained
with only Skull, she began to say that her father had
been telling her to marry a man, but she did not listen
to or believe him.

When the lady saw that the gentleman became a Skull,
she began to faint, but the Skull told her if she would die
she would die and she would follow him to his house.
But by the time that he was saying so, he was humming
with a terrible voice and also grew very wild and even if
there was a person two miles away he would not have to
listen before hearing him, so this lady began to run away
in that forest for her life, but the Skull chased her and
within a few yards, he caught her, because he was very
clever and smart as he was only Skull and he could jump
a mile to the second before coming down. He caught the
lady in this way: so when the lady was running away for

her life, he hastily ran to her front and stopped her as a log of wood.

By and by, this lady followed the Skull to his house, and the house was a hole which was under the ground. When they reached there both of them entered the hole. But there were only Skulls living in that hole. At the same time that they entered the hole, he tied a single Cowrie on the neck of this lady with a kind of rope, after that, he gave her a large frog on which she sat as a stool, then he gave a whistle to a Skull of his kind to keep watch on this lady whenever she wanted to run away. Because the Skull knew already that the lady would attempt to run away from the hole. Then he went to the backyard to where his family were staying in the daytime till night.

But one day, the lady attempted to escape from the hole, and at the same time that the Skull who was watching her whistled to the rest of the Skulls that were in the backyard, the whole of them rushed out to the place where the lady sat on the bull-frog, so they caught her, but as all of them were rushing out, they were rolling on the ground as if a thousand petrol drums were pushing along a hard road. After she was caught, then they brought her back to sit on the same frog as usual. If the Skull who was watching her fell asleep, and if the lady wanted to escape, the cowrie that was tied on her neck would raise up the alarm with a terrible noise, so that the Skull who was watching her would wake up at once and then the rest of the Skull's family would rush out from the back in thousands to the lady and ask her what she wanted to do with a curious and terrible voice.

But the lady could not talk at all, because as the cowrie had been tied on her neck, she became dumb at the same moment.

'THE FATHER OF GODS SHOULD FIND OUT WHEREABOUTS
   THE DAUGHTER OF THE HEAD OF THE TOWN WAS. . . .'

F

Now as the father of the lady first asked for my name and I told him that my name was 'Father of gods who could do anything in this world', then he told me that if I could find out where his daughter was and bring her to him, then he would tell me where my palm-wine tapster was. But when he said so, I was jumping up with gladness that he should promise me that he would tell me where my tapster was. I agreed to what he said; the father and parent of this lady never knew whereabouts their daughter was, but they had information that the lady followed a complete gentleman in the market. As I was the 'Father of gods who could do anything in this world', when it was at night I sacrificed to my juju with a goat.

And when it was early in the morning, I sent for forty kegs of palm-wine, after I has drunk it all, I started to investigate whereabouts was the lady. As it was the market-day, I started the investigation from the market. But as I was a juju-man, I knew all the kinds of people in that market. When it was exactly 9 o'clock a.m., the very complete gentleman whom the lady followed came to the market again, and at the same time I saw him, I knew that he was a curious and terrible creature.

'THE LADY WAS NOT TO BE BLAMED FOR FOLLOWING THE SKULL AS A COMPLETE GENTLEMAN' . . .

I could not blame the lady for following the Skull as a complete gentleman to his house at all. Because if I were a lady, no doubt I would follow him to wherever he would go, and still as I was a man I would jealous him more than that, because if this gentleman went to the battlefield, surely, enemy would not kill him or capture him, and if bombers saw him in a town which was to be bombed, they would not throw bombs on his presence, and if they did throw it, the bomb itself would not explode until this gentleman would leave that town, because of his beauty. At the same time that I saw this gentleman in the market on that day, what I was doing was only to follow him about the market. After I looked at him for so many hours, then I ran to a corner of the market and I cried for a few minutes because I thought within myself why was I not created with beauty as this gentleman, but when I remembered that he was only a Skull, then I thanked God that He had created me without beauty, so I went back to him in the market, but I was still attracted by his beauty. So when the market closed for that day, and when everybody was returning to his or her destination, this gentleman was returning to his own too and I followed him to know where he was living.

'INVESTIGATION TO THE SKULL'S FAMILY HOUSE'

When I travelled with him a distance of about twelve miles away to that market, the gentleman left the road on which we were travelling and branched into an endless forest and I was following him, but as I did not want him to see that I was following him, then I used one of my juju which changed me into a lizard and followed him. But after I had travelled with him a distance of about twenty-five miles away in this endless forest, he began to pull out all the parts of his body and return them to the owners, and paid them.

After I had travelled with him for another fifty miles in this forest, then he reached his house and entered it, but I entered it also with him, as I was a lizard. The first thing that he did when he entered the hole (house) he went straight to the place where the lady was, and I saw the lady sat on a bull-frog with a single cowrie tied on her neck and a Skull who was watching her stood behind her. After he (gentleman) had seen that the lady was there, he went to the backyard where all his family were working.

'THE INVESTIGATOR'S WONDERFUL WORK IN THE SKULL'S FAMILY HOUSE'

When I saw this lady and when the Skull who brought her to that hole of whom I followed from the market to that hole went to the back-yard, then I changed myself to a man as before, then I talked to the lady but she could not answer me at all, she only showed that she was in a serious condition. The Skull who was guarding her with a whistle fell asleep at that time

To my surprise, when I helped the lady to stand up from the frog on which she sat, the cowrie that was tied on her neck made a curious noise at once, and when the Skull who was watching her heard the noise, he woke up and blew the whistle to the rest, then the whole of them rushed to the place and surrounded the lady and me, but at the same time that they saw me there, one of them ran to a pit which was not so far from that spot, the pit was filled with cowries. He picked one cowrie out of the pit, after that he was running towards me, and the whole crowd wanted to tie the cowrie on my neck too. But before they could do that, I had changed myself into air, they could not trace me out again, but I was looking at them. I believed that the cowries in that pit were their power and to reduce the power of any human being whenever tied on his or her neck and also to make a person dumb.

Over one hour after I had dissolved into air, these Skulls went back to the back-yard, but there remained the Skull who was watching her.

After they had returned to the backyard, I changed to a man as usual, then I took the lady from the frog, but at the same time that I touched her, the cowrie which was tied on her neck began to shout; even if a person was four miles away he would not have to listen before hearing, but immediately the Skull who was watching her heard the noise and saw me when I took her from that frog, he blew the whistle to the rest of them who were in the backyard.

Immediately the whole Skull family heard the whistle when blew to them, they were rushing out to the place and before they could reach there I had left their hole for the forest, but before I could travel about one hundred yards in the forest, they had rushed out from their hole to inside the forest and I was still running away with the lady. As these Skulls were chasing me about in the forest, they were rolling on the ground like large stones and also humming with terrible noise, but when I saw that they had nearly caught me or if I continued to run away like that, no doubt, they would catch me sooner, then I changed the lady to a kitten and put her inside my pocket and changed myself to a very small bird which I could describe as a 'sparrow' in English language.

After that I flew away, but as I was flying in the sky, the cowrie which was tied on that lady's neck was still making a noise and I tried all my best to stop the noise, but all were in vain. When I reached home with the lady, I changed her to a lady as she was before and also myself changed to a man as well. When her father saw that I had brought his daughter back home, he was exceedingly glad and said thus: 'You are the "Father of gods" as you had told me before.'

But as the lady was now at home, the cowrie on her neck did not stop making a terrible noise once, and she could not talk to anybody; she showed only that she was very glad that she was at home. Now I had brought the lady but she could not talk, eat or loose away the cowrie on her neck, because the terrible noise of the cowrie did not allow anybody to rest or sleep at all.

OTHER BOOKS BY AMOS TUTUOLA

My Life in the Bush of Ghosts (Faber & Faber, 1954)
Simbi and the Satyr of the Dark Jungle (Faber & Faber, 1955)
The Brave African Huntress (Faber & Faber, 1958)
The Feather Woman of the Jungle (Faber & Faber, 1962)

CAMARA LAYE

CAMARA LAYE belongs to the Malinke people, and was born in French Guinea in 1924. After attending technical college in Conakry he went to Paris to train as an engineer. After three years his money ran out and he was forced to work in the large Simca factory. While here, lonely and poor, he wrote his first novel, *The Dark Child*. He followed this up with his second novel, *The Radiance of the King*.

The Dark Child, published in 1955, is essentially autobiographical. In this book Camara Laye traces his life from his childhood in Kouroussa, sitting in the yard of his father's goldsmith shop. Once at primary school he made annual visits to his grandmother at harvest time, and followed eagerly on the heels of his Uncle Lansana, the champion reaper of the village. He received his secondary education at the technical college at Conakry (400 miles from his home village on the Atlantic coast of Guinea) where he lived with his father's brother, an educated business man. After four years he received support to study further in Paris and subsequently set out. The following excerpt tells of happenings on the night when Camara must join the company of the uncircumcized and brave the terror of Kondén Diara, the 'lion that eats up little boys'.

The Night of Kondén Diara

I was growing up. The time had come for me to join the society of the initiated. This rather mysterious society

– and at that age, it was very mysterious to me, though not very secret – contained all the young boys, all the uncircumcized of twelve, thirteen or fourteen years of age, and it was run by our elders, whom we called the big 'Kondéns'. I joined it one evening before the feast of Ramadan.

As soon as the sun had gone down, the tom-tom had begun to beat. Even though it was being played in a remote part of the concessions, its notes had roused me at once, had struck my breast, had struck right at my heart, just as if Kodoké, our best player, had been playing for me alone. A little later, I had heard faintly the shrill voices of boys accompanying the tom-tom with their cries and singing. . . . Yes, the time had come for me. . . .

It was the first time I had spent the feast of Ramadan at Kouroussa; until this year, my grandmother had always insisted on my spending it with her, at Tindican. All that morning, and even more so in the afternoon, I had been in a state of great agitation, with everyone busy preparing for the festival, bumping into and pushing each other and asking me to help. Outside, the uproar was just as bad: Kouroussa is the chief town of our region, and all the canton chiefs, attended by their musicians, make it a custom to gather here for the festival. From the gateway to the concession I had watched them pass by, with their companies of praise-singers, balaphonists and guitarists, drum and tom-tom players. Until now I had only been thinking of the festival and of the sumptuous feast that awaited me – but now, there was something quite different in the wind.

The screaming crowd that surrounded Kodoké and his tom-tom was getting nearer. It was going from one concession to another; it would stop for a moment in each concession where there was a boy of an age, as I was, to join the society, and it would take the boy away. That is why it was so slow in coming, yet so sure, so ineluctable; as sure, as ineluctable as the fate that awaited me.

What fate? My meeting with 'Kondén Diara'.

Now I was not unaware who Kondén Diara was; often my mother, and at times my uncles, had talked of him only too much, had threatened me only too often with Kondén Diara, that terrible bogey man, 'that lion that eats up little boys'. And here was Kondén Diara – but was he a man? Was he an animal? Was he not rather half man, half animal? My friend Kouyaté believed he was more man than beast – here was Kondén Diara leaving the dim world of hearsay, here he was taking on flesh and blood, yes, and was prowling, roused by Kodoké's tom-tom, around the dark town! This night was to be the night of Kondén Diara.

I could hear now very plainly the beating of tom-tom – Kodoké was much nearer – I could hear perfectly the chanting and the shouts that rose into the dark, I could make out distinctly the rather hollow, crisp, well-marked beats of the coros, that are a kind of miniature canoe, and are beaten with a bit of wood. I was standing at the entrance to the concession, waiting. I, too, was holding ready to play it, my coro, with the stick clutched nervously in my hand; I was waiting, hidden by the shadow of the hut; I was waiting, filled with a dreadful anxiety, my eyes searching the blackness.

'Well?' asked my father.

He had crossed the workshop without my hearing him.

'Are you afraid?'

'A little,' I replied.

He laid his hands on my shoulder.

'It's all right. Don't worry.'

He drew me to him, and I could feel his warmth; it warmed me, too, and I began to feel less frightened, my heart did not beat so fast.

'I, too, went through this test,' said my father.

'What happened to you?' I asked.

'Nothing you need really be afraid of, nothing you cannot overcome by your own will-power. Remember; you have to control your fear, you have to control yourself. Kondén Diara will not take you away; he will roar; but he won't do more than roar. You won't be frightened, now, will you?'

'I'll try not to be.'

'Even if you are frightened, do not show it.'

He went away, and I began waiting again, and the disturbing uproar came nearer and nearer. Suddenly I saw the crowd emerging from the dark and rushing towards me; Kodoké, his tom-tom slung over one shoulder, was marching at their head, followed by the drummers.

I ran back quickly into the yard, and, standing in the middle of it, I awaited, with as much pluck as I could muster, the awful invasion. I did not have long to wait; the crowd was upon me, it was spreading tumultuously all around me, overwhelming me with shouts and cries and beating tom-toms, beating drums. It formed a circle and I found myself in the centre, alone, curiously isolated, still free and yet already captive. Inside the circle, I recognized Kouyaté and others, many of them friends of mine who had been collected as the crowd moved on, collected as I was to be, as I already was; and it seemed to me they were none of them looking very happy – but was I any more than they were? I began to beat my coro, as they were doing; perhaps I was beating it with less confidence than they.

At this point young girls and women joined the circle and began to dance; young men and adolescents, stepping out of the crowd, moved into the circle too and began to dance facing the women. The men sang, the women clapped their hands. Soon the only ones left to form the circle were the uncircumcised boys. They, too, began to sing – they were not allowed to dance – and as they sang,

sang in unison, they forgot their anxiety; I, too, mingled my voice with theirs. When, having formed a circle again, the crowd left our concession, I went with it, almost willingly beating my coro with great enthusiasm. Kouyaté was on my right.

Towards the middle of the night, our tour of the town and the collection of uncircumcized boys was finished – we had arrived at the farthest outskirts of the concessions, and in front of us lay only the dark shrub-land. Here the women and young girls left us – then the grown men left us. We were alone with the older boys, or should I say 'delivered over' to the older boys – for I remember the often rather disagreeable natures and rarely pleasant manners of those older ones.

The women and young girls now hurried back to their dwellings. Actually, they cannot have been any more at ease than we were; I know for a fact that not one of them would have ventured to leave town on this night. In a short while, when Kondén Diara would begin to roar, they would not be able to stop shaking with fright; they would all be shaking in their shoes, and making sure the doors were all properly barred. For them, as for us, though in a much less significant way, this night would be the night of Kondén Diara.

As soon as our elders had made sure that no intruder was present to disturb the seriousness of the ceremony, we left the town behind and entered the bush by a path which leads to a sacred place where each year the initiation takes place. The place is well known; it is situated under an enormous bambox tree, a hollow at the junction of the River Komoni and the River Niger. At normal times, it is forbidden to go there; but certainly it had not always been so, an emanation from the past I never knew still seems to hover around the huge trunk of the bombax tree; I think that a night such as the one we were going through must certainly have resurrected a part of that past.

We were walking in silence, closely hemmed in by our elders. Perhaps they were afraid we might escape? It looked like it. I do not think, however, that the idea of escape had occurred to any of us; the night, and that particular night, seem impenetrable. Who knew where Kondén Diara had his lair? Who knew where he was prowling? But was it not right here near the hollow? Yes, it must be here. And if we had to face him – and certainly we had to face him – it would surely be better to do so in a crowd, in this jostling group that seemed to make us all one, and seemed like a last refuge from the peril that was approaching.

Nevertheless, however intimate our jostling proximity to one another, and however careful the vigilance of our elders, it could not be denied that the silence of our progress, after the recent uproar, as we marched far from the huts through the wan moonlight, and even more, the thought of the sacred place towards which we were going, and, finally and above all, the concealed presence of Kondén Diara – all these things filled us with terror.

Just before we reached the hollow, we saw flames leap up from a huge wood fire that the bushes had hidden from us until then. Kouyaté squeezed my arm and I knew he was referring to the fire. I quickened my steps – we all quickened our steps – and the crimson radiance of the fire enveloped us. We had a harbour now, a kind of haven from the night: a huge blaze, and, at our backs, the bombax tree's enormous trunk. Oh! it was a precarious haven! But, however poor, it was infinitely better than the silence and the dark, the sullen silence of the dark. We assembled beneath the bombax tree. The ground beneath had been cleared of reeds and tall grasses.

Our elders suddenly shouted, 'Kneel!'

We at once fell to our knees.

'Heads down!'

We lowered our heads.

'Lower than that!'

We bent our heads right to the ground, as if in prayer.

'Now hide your eyes!'

We don't have to be told twice; we shut our eyes tight and press our hands over them. For would we not die of fright and horror if we should see, or so much as catch a glimpse of Kondén Diara? Our elders walk up and down, behind us and in front of us, to make sure that we have all obeyed their orders to the letter. Woe to him who would have the audacity to disobey! He would be cruelly whipped.

Now that we are on our knees with our foreheads to the ground and our hands pressed over our eyes, Kondén Diara's roaring suddenly bursts out.

We were expecting to hear this hoarse roar, we were not expecting any other sound, but it takes us by surprise, and shatters us, freezes our hearts with its unexpectedness. And it is not only a lion, it is not only Kondén Diara roaring: there are ten, twenty, perhaps thirty lions that take their lead from him, uttering their terrible roars and surrounding the hollow; ten or thirty lions separated from us by a few yards only and that the great wood fire will perhaps not always keep at bay; lions of every size and every age – we can tell that by the way they roar – from the very oldest lions to the very youngest cubs. No, not one of us would dream of venturing to open an eye, not one! Not one of us would dare to lift his head from the ground: he would rather bury it in the earth. And I bend down as far as I can: we all bend down farther, we bend our knees as much as we can, we keep our backs as low as possible; I make myself, we all make ourselves as small as we can.

'You must not be afraid!' I told myself. 'You must conquer your fear! Your father told you to overcome your fear!' But how could I not be afraid? Even inside the town, far from this clearing, women and children were tremb-

ling and crouching in their huts; they were listening to
Kondén Diara roaring, many of them were stopping their
ears so as not to hear him roaring; a few bolder spirits
might be getting up – it needs some courage to leave one's
bed just now – to make quite sure that their hut door is
closed, to make quite sure that it is securely bolted and
barred; nevertheless they are still as frightened as anyone
else. How can I possibly not give way to my terror, I who
am within reach of this monster? If it so pleased him, he
could leap right through the fire and plunge his terrible
claws into my flesh!

Not for a single instant do I doubt the presence of the
monster. Who could assemble such a numerous herd, hold
such a nocturnal revel, if not Kondén Diara? 'He alone,'
I said to myself, 'he alone has such power over lions. . . .
Keep away, Kondén Diara! Keep away! Go back into
the bush! . . .' But Kondén Diara went on with his revels,
and sometimes it seemed to me that he roared right over
my own head, right in my own ears even. 'Keep away,
I implore thee, Kondén Diara!'

What was it my father had said? 'Kondén Diara roars;
but he won't do more than roar; he will not take you
away. . . .' Yes, something like that. But is it true, really
true? There is also a rumour that Kondén Diara sometimes pounces with fearsome claws on someone or other
and carries him far away, far, far away into the depths of
the bush; and then, days and days afterwards, months or
even years later, quite by chance a huntsman may discover some whitened bones. . . . And do not people also
die of fright? . . . Ah! how I wish this roaring would stop!
How I wish . . . How I wish I was far away from this
clearing, back in the concession, in the warm security of
the hut! . . . Will this roaring never end? . . . Go away,
Kondén Diara! Go away! . . . Stop roaring. . . . Oh, those
roars! . . . I feel as if I can bear them no longer. . . .

Whereupon, suddenly they stop! They stop just as they

had begun, so suddenly, in fact, that I feel only reluctant relief. Is it over? Really over? Is it not just a temporary interruption? . . . No, I dare not feel relieved just yet. And then suddenly the voice of one of the older boys rings out:

'Get up!'

I heave a sigh of relief. This time, it's really over. We look at one another. I look at Kouyaté and the others. If there were only a little more light . . . But the light from the fire is sufficient: great drops of sweat are still beading our foreheads: yet the night is chill. . . . Yes, we were afraid. We were not able to conceal our fear. . . .

A new command rang out, and we sat down in front of the fire. Now our elders begin our initiation; all night long they will teach us the songs of the uncircumcized; and we must remain quite still, repeating the words after them, singing the melody after them; there we sit, as if we were in school again, attentive, very attentive, and very obedient.

Our lessons ended with the dawn.

My legs and arms were numb; I worked my joints and rubbed my legs for a while, but my blood still flowed slowly; I was really worn out, and I was cold. Looking round me, I could not understand why I shook with fear during the night: the first rays of dawn were falling so gently, so reassuringly, on the bombax tree, on the clearing; the sky looked so pure! Who could believe that only a few hours ago a whole herd of lions, led by Kondén Diara himself, had been angrily roaring among these tall reeds and grasses, separated from us only by a wood fire which now was almost dead? No one would have believed it, and I should have doubted the evidence of my own ears and thought I was waking up from a bad dream, if one or the other of my companions had not now and then cast a suspicious glance at the tallest grasses.

NOTES

Ramadan : the month throughout which Moslems are required
   to fast from dawn to sunset
concession : a household in Guinea
canton : district
balaphonists : men who blow musical instruments

ALSO BY CAMARA LAYE
The Radiance of the King (Collins, 1956)

JAMES MATTHEWS

JAMES MATTHEWS was born in Cape Town in 1929. Eldest son of a poor and large family, his first job was as a newspaper-seller while still at school. After leaving High School he was in turn messenger, journalist, and is at present a telephonist. His collection of short stories, *Azikwewla*, has been published in Sweden.

In his short story, *The Park*, James Matthews tells of the frustration of a little coloured boy living in poverty, who is denied the right to play in the Park reserved for white children. He sketches one day in the life of a child in the Cape Town slums.

The Park

He looked longingly at the children on the other side of the railings; the children sliding down the chute, landing with feet astride on the bouncy lawn; screaming as they almost touched the sky with each upward curve of their swings; their joyful, demented shrieks at each dip of the merry-go-round. He looked at them and his body trembled and itched to share their joy – buttocks to fit board, and hands and feet to touch steel. Next to him, on the ground, was a bundle of clothing, washed and ironed, wrapped in a sheet.

Five small boys, pursued by two bigger ones, ran past,

He looked longingly at the children at the other side of the railings

ignoring him. One of the bigger boys stopped. 'What are you looking at, you brown ape?' he said, stooping to pick up a lump of clay. He recognized him. The boy was present the day he was put out of the park. The boy pitched the lump, shattering it on the rail above his head and the fragments fell on to his face.

He spat out the particles of clay clinging to the lining of his lips, eyes searching for an object to throw at the boys separated from him by the railings. More boys joined the one in front of him and he was frightened by their number.

Without a word he shook his bundle free from the clay and raised it to his head and walked away.

As he walked he recalled his last visit to the park. Without hesitation he had gone through the gates and got on to the nearest swing. Even now he could feel that pleasurable thrill which travelled the length of his body as he rocketed himself higher, higher, until he felt that the swing would up-end him when it reached its peak. Almost leisurely he had allowed it to come to a halt, like a pendulum shortening its stroke, and then ran towards the see-saw. A white boy, about his own age, was seated opposite him. Accordion-like, their legs folded to send the see-saw jerking from the indentation it pounded in the grass. A hand pressing on his shoulder stopped a jerk. He turned around to look into the face of the attendant.

'Get off!' The skin tightened between his eyes. 'Why must I get off? What have I done?' He held on, hands clamped on to the iron hoop attached to the wooden see-saw. The white boy jumped off from the other end and stood – a detached spectator. 'You must get off!' The attendant spoke in a low voice so that it would not carry to the people who were gathering.

'The council says,' he continued, 'that we coloureds must not use the same swings as the whites. You must use the park where you stay.' His voice apologizing for the uniform he wore which gave him the right to be in the park to watch that the little whites were not hurt while playing.

'There's no park where we stay.' He waved a hand in the direction of a block of flats. 'There's a park on the other side of town but I don't know where it is.' He walked past them. The mothers with their babies – pink and belching – cradled in their arms, the children lolling on the grass, his companion from the see-saw, the nurse girls – their uniforms their badges of indemnity – pushing prams. Beside him walked the attendant. At the entrance, the attendant pointed an accusing finger at a notice board.

'There you can read for yourself.' Absolving himself of any blame. He struggled with the red letters on the white background.

'Blankes Alleen, Whites Only.' He walked through the gates and behind him the swings screeched, the see-saw rattled, and the merry-go-round rumbled.

He walked past the park as on each occasion after that he had been forced to walk past it.

He shifted the bundle to a more comfortable position, easing the pain biting into his shoulder muscles. What harm would I be doing if I were to use the swings? Would it stop the swings from swinging? Would the chute collapse? The bundle pressed deeper and the pain became an even line across his shoulders and he had no answer to his reasoning.

The park itself, with its wide lawns and flower-beds and rockeries and dwarf trees, meant nothing to him. It was the gaily painted tubing, the silver chains and brown boards, transport to never-never land, which gripped him.

Only once, long ago, and then almost as if by mistake, had he been on something to beat it. He was taken by his father, in one of those rare moments when they were taken anywhere, to a fair ground. He had stood captivated by the wooden horses with their gilded reins and scarlet saddles dipping in time to the music as they whirled by.

For a brief moment he was astride one and he prayed it would last for ever, but the moment lasted only the time it took him to whisper the prayer. Then he was standing, clutching his father's trousers, watching the other riders astride the dipping horses.

Another shifting of the bundle and he was at the house where he delivered the clothing his mother had washed in a round tub, filled with boiling water, the steam covering her face with a film of sweat. Her voice, when she spoke, was as soft and clinging as the steam enveloping her.

He pushed the gate open and walked around the back, watching for the aged lap-dog which, at his entry, would rush out to wheeze asthmatically around his feet and nip with blunt teeth at his ankles.

A round-faced African girl, her blackness heightened by the white, starched uniform she wore, opened the kitchen door to let him in. She cleared the table and placed the bundle on it.

'I will call madam.' She said the words spaced and highly pitched as if she had some difficulty in uttering the syllables in English. Her buttocks bounced beneath the tight uniform and the backs of her calves shone with fat.

'Are you sure you've brought everything?' was the greeting he received each time he brought the bundle, and each time she checked every item and always nothing was missing. He looked at her and lowered his voice as he said, 'Everything's there, madam.'

What followed had become a routine between the three of them.

'Have you had anything to eat?' she asked him.

He shook his head.

'Well, we can't let you go off like that.' Turning to the African woman in the white, starched uniform, 'What have we got?'

The maid swung open the refrigerator door and took

out a plate of food. She placed it on the table and set a glass of milk next to it.

When he was seated the white woman left the kitchen and he was alone with the maid.

His nervousness left him and he could concentrate on what was on the plate.

A handful of peas, a dab of mashed potato, a tomato sliced into bleeding circles, a sprinkling of grated carrots, and no rice.

White people are funny, he told himself. How can anyone fill himself with this? It doesn't form a lump, like the food my mama makes.

He washed it down with milk.

'Thank you, Annie,' he said as he pushed the glass aside.

Her teeth gleamed porcelain-white as she smiled.

He sat fidgeting, impatient to be outside, away from the kitchen with its glossy, tiled floor and steel cupboards Duco-ed a clinical white to match the food-stacked refrigerator.

'I see you have finished.' The voice startled him. She held out an envelope containing the ten-shilling note – payment for his mother's weekly struggle over the wash tub. 'This is for you.' A sixpence was dropped into his hand, a long fingernail raking his palm.

'Thank you, madam.' His voice barely audible.

'Tell your mother I'm going away on holiday for about a month and I will let her know when I'm back.'

Then he was dismissed and her high heels tapped out of the kitchen. He nodded his head at the African maid who took an apple from the bowl which was bursting with fruit, and handed it to him.

Her smile bathed her face in light.

As he walked down the path he finished off the apple with big bites.

Before he reached the gate the dog was after him, its hot breath warming his heels. He turned and poked his toes into its face. It barked hoarsely in protest, a look of outrage on its face.

He laughed delightedly at the expression which changed the dog's features into those of an old man.

Let's see you do that again. He waved his foot in front of the pug-nose. The nose retreated and made an about-turn, waddling away with its dignity deflated by his affront.

As he walked he mentally spent his sixpence.

I'll buy a penny drops, the sour ones which taste like limes; a penny bull's eyes, a packet of sherbet with the licorice tube at the end of the packet; and a penny star toffees, red ones, which colour your tongue and turn your spittle into blood.

His glands were titillated and his mouth filled with saliva. He stopped at the first shop and walked inside.

Trays were filled with expensive chocolates and sweets of a type never seen in jars on the shelves of the Indian shop at the corner where he stayed. He walked out, not buying a thing.

His footsteps lagged as he reached the park.

The nurse girls with their babies and prams were gone, their places occupied by old men, who, with their hands holding up their stomachs, were casting disapproving eyes over the confusion and clatter confronting them.

A ball was kicked perilously close to one old man, and the boy who ran after it stopped as the old man raised his stick, daring him to come closer.

The rest of them called to the boy to get the ball. He edged closer and made a grab at it as the old man swung his cane. The cane missed him by more than a foot and he swaggered back, the ball held under his arm. Their game was resumed.

From the other side of the railings he watched them; the boys kicking the ball; the children cavorting on the grass; even the old men, senile on the seats; but most of all, the children enjoying themselves with what was denied him; and his whole body yearned to be part of them.

'Damn it!' He looked over his shoulder to see if anyone had heard him. 'Damn it!' he said louder. 'Damn on them! Their park, the grass, the swings, the see-saw. Everything! Damn it! Damn it!'

His small hands impotently shook the tall railings towering above his head.

It struck him that he would not be seeing the park for a whole month, that there would be no reason for him to pass it.

Despair filled him. He had to do something to ease his anger.

A bag filled with fruit peelings was on top of the rubbish stacked in a waste-basket fitted to a pole. He reached for it and frantically threw it over the railings. He ran without waiting to see the result.

Out of breath three streets farther, he slowed down, pain stabbing beneath his heart. The act had brought no relief, only intensified the longing.

He was oblivious of the people passing, the hoots of the vehicles whose path he crossed without thinking. Once, when he was roughly pushed aside, he did not even bother to look and see who had done it.

The familiar shrieks and smells told him he was home.

The Indian shop could not draw him out of his melancholy mood and he walked past it, his sixpence unspent, in his pocket.

A group of boys were playing on the pavement.

Some of them called to him but he ignored them and turned into a short side-street.

He mounted the flat stoep of a double-storey house with a façade that must have been painted once but had now turned a nondescript grey with the red brick underneath showing through.

Beyond the threshold the room was dim. He walked

past the scattered furniture with a familiarity that did not
need guidance.

His mother was in the kitchen, hovering above a pot
perched on a pressure stove.

He placed the envelope on the table. She put aside the
spoon and stuck a finger under the flap of the envelope,
tearing it in half. She placed the ten-shilling note in a
spoutless teapot on the shelf.

'Are you hungry?'

He nodded his head.

She poured him a cup of soup and added a thick slice
of brown bread.

Between bites of bread and sips of the soup which
scalded his throat he told her that there wouldn't be any
washing coming during the week.

'Why? What's the matter? What have I done?'

'Nothing. Madam says she's going away for a month
and she'll let mama know when she gets back.'

'What am I going to do now?' Her voice took on a
whine and her eyes strayed to the teapot containing the
money. The whine hardened to reproach as she continued.
'Why didn't she let me know she was going away? I could
have looked for another madam.'

She paused. 'I slave away and the pain never leaves
my back, and it's too much for her to let me know she's
going away. The money I get from her just keeps us nicely
steady. How am I going to cover the hole?'

As he ate, he wondered how the ten shillings he had
brought helped to keep them nicely steady. There was no
change in their meals. It was, as usual, not enough and
the only time they received new clothes was at Christmas.

'There's the burial to pay and I was going to ask Mr
Lemonsky to bring some lino for the front room. I'm sick
of seeing boards where the lino's worn through, but it's
no use asking him to bring it now. Without money you
have as much hope as getting wine on a Saturday.'

He hurried his eating to get away from the words wafting towards him, before they could soak into him, trapping him in the chair to witness his mother's miseries.

Outside, they were still playing with their tyres. He joined them half-heartedly. As he rolled the tyre, his spirit was in the park on the swings. There was no barrier to his coming and he could do as he pleased. He was away from the narrow streets and squawking children and speeding cars. He was in a place of green grass and red tubing and silver steel. The tyre rolled past him. He made no effort to grab it.

'Go get the tyre.' ... 'Are you asleep?' ... 'Don't you want to play any more?' He walked away, ignoring their cries.

Rage boiled up inside him. Rage against the houses with their streaked walls and smashed panes filled by too many people; the overflowing garbage pails outside doors; the alleys and streets; and a law he could not understand; a law that shut him out of the park.

He burst into tears. He swept his arms across his cheeks to check his weeping.

He lowered his hands to peer at the boy confronting him.

'I'm not crying, damn you. Something's gone into my eye and I was rubbing it.'

'I think you're crying.'

He pushed past and continued towards the shop. 'Crying doll!' the boy's taunt rang after him.

The shop's sole, iron-barred window was crowded. Oranges were mixed with writing paper and dried figs were strewn on school slates; clothing and crockery collected dust. Across the window a cockroach made its leisurely way, antennae on the alert.

Inside, the shop was as crowded as the window. Bags covered the floor, leaving a narrow path to the counter. 'Yes, boy?' He showed teeth scarlet with betel.

'Come'n, boy. What you want? No stand here all day.' His jaws worked at the betel-nut held captive by his stained teeth.

He ordered penny portions of his selections.

Transferring the sweets to his pocket he threw the torn container on the floor and walked out. Behind him the Indian murmured grimly, jaws working faster.

One side of the street was in shadow. He sat with his back against the wall, savouring the last of the sun.

Bull's-eye, peppermint, a piece of licorice – all lumped together in his cheek. For the moment, the park was forgotten.

He watched the girl advance without interest.

'Mama says you must come 'n eat.' She stared at his bulging cheek, one hand rubbing the side of her nose. 'Gimme.' He gave her a bull's-eye which she dropped into her mouth between dabs at her nose.

'Wipe your snot!' he ordered her, showing his superiority. He walked past. She followed, sucking and sniffing.

When they entered the kitchen their father was already seated at the table.

'Why must I always send somebody after you?' his mother said.

He slipped into his seat and then hurriedly got up to wash his hands before his mother could find fault with yet another point.

Supper was a silent affair except for the scraping of spoon across plate and an occasional sniff from his sister.

Almost at the end of the meal a thought came to mind. He sat, spoon poised in the air, shaken by its magnitude. Why not go to the park after dark? After it had closed its gates on the old men, the children, the nurses with their prams. There would be no one to stop him. He couldn't think further. He was light-headed with the thought of it. His mother's voice, as she related her day to his father, was not the steam which stung but a soft breeze wafting past him, leaving him undisturbed. Qualms troubled him. He had never been in that part of town at night. A band of fear tightened across his chest, contracting his insides, making it hard for him to swallow his food. He gripped his spoon more tightly, stretching the skin across his knuckles.

I'll do it! I'll go to the park as soon as we're finished eating. He controlled himself with difficulty. He swallowed what was left on his plate and furtively checked to see how the others were faring. Hurry it up! Hurry it up!

When his father pushed the last plate aside and lit a cigarette, he hastily cleared the table and began washing up.

Each piece of crockery washed, he passed on to his sister whose sniffing kept pace with their combined operation.

The dishes done, he swept the kitchen and carried out the garbage bin.

'Can I go out and play, mama?'

'Don't let me have to send for you again.'

His father remained silent, buried behind his newspaper.

'Before you go,' his mother stopped him, 'light the lamp and hang it in the passage.'

He filled the lamp with paraffin, turned up its wick and lit it. The light glimmered weakly through the streaked glass.

The moon to him was a fluorescent ball – light without warmth – and the stars, fragments chipped off it. Beneath street lights card games were in session. As he walked past, he sniffed the nostril-prickling smell of dagga. Dim doorways could not conceal couples clutching at each other.

Once clear of the district he broke into a jog-trot. He did not slacken his pace as he passed through downtown with its wonderland shop windows. As he neared the park his elation seeped out and his footsteps dragged.

In front of him was the park with its gate and iron

railings. Behind the railings stood impaled the notice board. He could see the swings beyond. The sight strengthened him.

He walked over, his breath coming faster. There was no one in sight. A car turned the corner and came towards him and he started at the sound of its engine. The car swept past, the tyres softly licking the asphalt.

The railings were icy-cold to his touch and the shock sent him into action. He extended his arms and with monkey-like movements pulled himself up to perch on top of the railings, then dropped on the newly-turned earth.

The grass was damp with dew and he swept his feet across it. Then he ran and the wet grass bowed beneath his bare feet.

He ran from the swings to the merry-go-round, see-saw to chute, hands covering the metal.

Up the steps to the top of the chute. He stood outlined against the sky. He was a bird, an eagle. He flung himself down on his stomach, sliding swiftly. Wheeeeeeeeh! He rolled over when he slammed on to the grass. He was looking at the moon for an instant, then propelled himself to his feet and ran for the steps of the chute to recapture that feeling of flight. Each time he swept down the chute he wanted the trip never to end, to go on sliding, sliding, sliding.

He walked reluctantly past the see-saw, consoling him-himself with pushing at one end to send it wacking on the grass.

'Damn it!' he grunted as he strained to set the merry-go-round in motion. Thigh tensed, leg stretched, he pushed. The merry-go-round moved. He increased his exertion and jumped on, one leg trailing at the ready, to shove if it should slow down. The merry-go-round dipped and swayed. To keep it moving, he had to push more than he rode. Not wanting to spoil his pleasure he jumped off and raced for the swings.

Feet astride, hands clutching silver chains, he jerked his body to gain momentum. He crouched like a runner, then violently straightened. The swing widened its arc. It swept higher, higher, higher. It reached the sky. He could touch the moon. He plucked a star to pin to his breast. The earth was far below him. No bird could fly as high as he. Upwards and onwards he went.

A light switched on in the hut at the far side of the park. It was a small patch of yellow on a dark square. The door opened and he saw a dark figure in the doorway, then the door was shut and the figure strode towards him. He knew it was the attendant. A torch glinted brightly in the moonlight, as it swung at his side.

He continued swinging.

The attendant came to a halt in front of him, out of reach of the swing's arc, and flashed his torch. The light caught him in mid-air.

'God-dammit!' the attendant swore, 'I've told you before you can't get on the swings.'

The rattle of chains when the boy shifted his feet was the only answer he received.

'Why did you come back?'

'The swings. I came back for the swings.'

The attendant catalogued the things denied them because of their colour. Even his job depended on their goodwill.

'Blerry whites! They got everything.'

All his feelings urged him to leave the boy alone, to let him continue to enjoy himself. But the fear that someone might see them hardened him.

'Get off! Go home!' he screamed, his voice harsh, his anger directed at the system that drove him against his own. 'If you don't get off, I'll go for the police. You know what they'll do to you.'

The swing raced back and forth.

The attendant turned and raced towards the gate.

'Mama. Mama.' His lips trembled, wishing himself safe in his mother's kitchen sitting next to the still-burning stove with a comic spread across his knees. 'Mama. Mama.' His voice mounted, wrenching from his throat, keeping pace with the soaring swing as it climbed to the sky. Voice and swing. Swing and voice. Higher. Higher. Higher. Until they were one.

At the entrance to the park the notice board stood tall, its shadow elongated, pointing towards him.

ALSO BY JAMES MATTHEWS

Azikwelwa (short stories) (Cavefors, 1962)

ALF WANNENBURGH

ALF WANNENBURGH was born in Cape Town in 1936. After matriculating he worked as a land-surveyor's assistant, salesman, clerk and window-dresser. He started writing articles and then turned to short stories. He is at present a student at the University of Cape Town.

The story is set immediately after the Coalbrook mine disaster in South Africa in which more than 400 people perished. Three men, impatient at the prospect of having to wait for transport back to their homes, decide to walk, and this ends in disaster for one of them.

Echoes

Three men stood in the dust and looked up at the road-sign.

'In two days we shall be in our home country,' said Tsolo.

Tsolo, Maki and Temba had been many days on the road to the Valley of a Thousand Hills. During the day they walked in the yellow dirt beneath the sun, and at night they lighted their fires beside the road and allowed their weariness to drain into the thirsting earth. They spoke little, for the horror of the place they had left remained with them.

More than four hundred of their fellow miners had died
in the disaster, and, after three weeks of vain efforts to
reach those who had been cut off from them by the fall
of rock, a funereal quiet had fallen over the workings. The
silent, the sullen, the weeping, the bewildered wives and
relatives, who had pressed around the fence, had gone,
and in their place torn newspapers were impaled on the
wire barbs by the wind. The silent winding gear cut a
stark silhouette against the grey sky, and the activity of the
compound became the despairing preparation for depar-
ture, of a refugee transit camp.

'The heat of this sun is heavy on our shoulders, like the
burden of the white man's laws,' said Tsolo, freeing his
arms and dropping his pack in the dust at his feet.

'Or like the suffering of our people at the mine,' said
Maki.

'There are some things we should not speak of,' said
Tsolo. 'We will change the laws of the white man, but the
suffering at the mine can never be changed.'

For a moment they were silent because it was with
sadness that they remembered the suffering at the mine.

'Let us stay here for the night so that we shall be strong
for the walk tomorrow,' said Temba.

'No, rather we should walk through the night, because
then we shall be home by tomorrow evening,' said Maki.
'Now that I am almost home, my legs are strong and
know no tiredness.'

'We *will* stay here,' said Tsolo.

He led the way through a break in the fence, and they
followed him into the deeply-etched, dry river-bed.

And that was the way it had always been. Tsolo was the
leader. When they had been at home together, it had been
Tsolo who led them to plough; and when the inadequate
soil had become poor and the crops had failed, they had

followed him to the labour-recruiting office. Once they had followed him to prison. But that had been a long time ago. His will was the strongest. And that was the way it had always been.

'This is a good place,' said Tsolo, dropping his blankets in the sand at the foot of the steep bank.

'It would be better if we went where the river turns, and where we cannot be seen from the road,' said Maki. 'In this place there is danger!'

There was a silence, and then his voice returned: 'there is danger . . . is danger . . . danger. . . .'

'Who is it that mocks us?' said Maki.

'It is a trick of the hills,' Tsolo replied.

Temba placed his blanket roll firmly beside that of Tsolo. 'This is a good place,' he agreed.

So they sat for a while in the fading warmth of the sand and watched the shadow of the bank creep across the river-bed.

It was Tsolo who spoke first: 'Do you remember that we came through a fence to get here?'

'Yes,' said Temba. 'It was you who found the opening for us.'

'And what does it mean that we came through a fence?'

'It means that we are on the land of a white farmer.'

'Now, if I tell you that my stomach is making the rumbling sounds of hunger?'

'Then I would say that on a farm such as this there are sheep.'

'Ah! you are a good fellow, Temba. How shall I say . . .? A good fellow,' Tsolo said, slapping Temba on the back. 'Yes, a *very* good fellow.'

Temba felt good. 'It is from you that I have learnt these things,' he said.

Their talk sounded faintly in the background of Maki's thoughts. He thought of the joy of the home-coming that

G

was before him, and the sorrow of the place that lay behind him; of his escape from the falling rocks that had entombed the miners, and of the talk that it had happened because of the white mine-owners, those who had not provided for their safety. He thought, too, of his friend, Moses, yes Moses, who had lost his life in the disaster, only two days before he was due to leave the mine; two days before he was to return to his family. Only two days. Of how happy he had been, and of the laughter in his eyes when he had spoken of his home. And then there had been a sound like the report of a great gun, and the ceiling of the mine had fallen on his dreams.

Then he remembered the first few days when they had laboured with hope, and the many days that followed, when they struggled to clear the broken earth with hope.

But mostly he thought of home, and of the anxious period of waiting, while those who were returning to Mozambique boarded their trains, when the three of them knew that their wives would have heard of the sadness that had come to the mine and would worry for their safety. Then they had been told that they would have to wait a further two weeks for transport to their home-country, and Tsolo had rolled up his blankets and spoken. And they followed him.

'He is a dreamer, this Maki,' said Tsolo.

'Yes, and a fool, for when we speak of sheep, we are speaking of *food*,' said Temba.

'You want me to worry with food when my mind is filled with much bigger things,' said Maki. 'In two days I shall be home with my wife. My son will ask me to tell him stories of the things I have seen. We shall sit beside the fire, and then I shall tell him of the painful things that I have seen. In being with my family there is far greater pleasure than in answering the squeals of my stomach. Am I, therefore, a dreamer?'

'What you have learnt of life is like nothing!' said Tsolo.

'You have learnt to cut coal and to dream, but you have learnt no wisdom.' He spoke with the bitter dust of the road in his voice.

'We cannot live on dreams,' said Temba.

'You speak of *home*,' said Tsolo. 'But what is this *home* if it is not a patch of poor soil on which our families must starve if we do not find work on the mines so that we can send money to our children? And you speak of this *home* as if it were Heaven! You are a dreamer, just like the one at the mine who was called Moses.'

'Yes, you are like Moses!' shouted Temba.

And the hills repeated: 'You are like Moses . . . are like Moses . . . like Moses. . . .'

'I do not like this place. We should leave, for even the hills mock us for this talk of stealing sheep when we should be on the road,' said Maki.

'Ah! so now our dreamer is afraid of an echo,' jeered Temba.

'Come,' said Tsolo. 'Let us leave him to his dreams or his fears; there is *men's* work for us to do.'

'But why should we do this thing now when we are so near to home?' said Maki. 'We may be caught, and then it will be many days before we can continue on our path. These farmers fear us because they are ignorant of us. This fear sometimes causes them to do terrible things to us.'

'I have my knife ready, let us find a sheep,' said Temba.

'Yes, then let us go,' said Tsolo. 'Maki, you will make the fire for us while we are gone.'

'If we are caught, it will be many days!' he shouted after them as they moved beyond the lip of the bank.

And *they* did not reply. But the hills answered: 'It will be many days . . . be many days . . . many days . . .'

Then darkness and silence came to the bed of the river, and the cold breeze of solitude was chill upon him. Beyond the towering blackness of the opposite bank.

filtered light, from an invisible moon, wove the fabric of the sky with blue threads. He gathered the driftwood of a long-past flood, and heaped it against a boulder in the sandy centre of the place where the stream had been.

In the warmth of the flames he felt the companionship of his family. If he excluded all else, the dancing yellow forms created about him the walls of his hut, the gentle love of his wife, and he heard the thirsty questions of his son beside him. And he planned how he would tell him of the many long roads he had traversed to be with him.

'And *still* he is dreaming!' the voice of Tsolo scorned from out of the dark.

Maki shook himself free of his thoughts as the two figures stepped into the light: first Tsolo, carrying the knife, and then Temba, with the carcass of a sheep slung over his shoulder.

'Ha!' said Temba. 'He has not even watched the fire well – must it also die?'

'Take this,' said Tsolo, handing Maki the knife. 'We men have done our work – now it is for one with the heart of a woman to prepare the sheep for the cooking.'

'But if we are found with the blood of this sheep on our hands, we shall not reach home!' said Maki.

'Must we not eat if we are to have strength for the journey tomorrow?' said Temba.

'You *dream* of danger – there is no one here,' jeered Tsolo.

And the hills confirmed: 'There is no one here . . . is no one here . . . no one here. . . .'

With the knife in his hand, Maki stood erect before the glowing coals. 'My strength does not come from that which belongs to other men,' he said.

Tsolo became angry. 'Do we not cut coal so that they become rich? Do we not build roads so that they can drive on them, while we must walk? Has not everything that we have been taken from us? You worry because we take this sheep. They have taken all from us – even our strength.'

'But I am already strong,' shouted Maki, 'because I am almost home!'

From the bank above them came a challenge and the sharp crack of a shotgun.

Tsolo and Temba fled from the light and vanished into the blackness where the river turned out of sight of the road.

Just beyond the ragged circle of firelight, illuminated by the weakening flare, lay three bundles of blankets; and beside the fire, two crumpled heaps: the sheep and Maki.

And the hills mocked: 'I am almost home ... am almost home ... almost home. ...'

WILLIAM CONTON

WILLIAM CONTON was born in Sierra Leone and afterwards became well known as a teacher and historian. He was in turn headmaster of Accra High School and Principal of the Government Secondary School at Bo. He is at present senior official of the Ministry of Education in Freetown. His novel, *The African* appeared in 1960.

The hero of *The African* is Kisimi Kamara. He is a young mission-educated Hausa, who leaves his native Songhai for England, where he receives a University degree. There he falls in love with a South African white girl, Greta, but returns to his native West Africa to become a successful politician. Greta dies, and he goes to South Africa to avenge her death. This excerpt shows Kisimi's early education in Sagresa, just prior to his earning a scholarship to England.

School at Sagresa

My new school was housed in a building which had been in turn a private house, a paupers' home, and a prison. Had we known at the time about all those interesting phases of the building's history, we might have invented a number of suitable jokes about it. But we did not; so we merely regarded the ungainly, thick-walled structure with a deep affection and reverence. It was large, as Sagresa buildings went then, standing in its own unpaved yard. The ground floor was a few feet below the level of the surrounding yard and the middle floor consisted of a big room which could be divided up by movable partitions into a variety of shapes for use as classrooms. The dormitories were on the top floor. At least three times as many rats as boys slept on that floor; but in due course the two parties achieved a state of peaceful coexistence. Housemasters also shared our accommodation under the corrugated roof, whilst the principal and his family lived in a house built onto the main school building, which also contained the chapel and the school printing press.

By English standards I suppose, and even by Sagresan standards, I would have been regarded as old to start a secondary education, for I must have been sixteen or seventeen at the time. By English standards, too, we would all have been considered 'swots'. We worked hard, without exception; for those who did not received short shrift from the masters. A ruler across the knuckles was the immediate penalty for obtuseness in class, and expulsion for bringing up the rear in the form order. Our basic fare included Greek (which we all loved) and mathematics, and these two subjects were also those in excelling at which we took the greatest pride. We saw very little of the principal, except in chapel, and what we saw of him made us take good care not to see more. He was tall and thin and possessed a vulture-beak nose. A punitive summons to his office was invariably followed by two or three days in the sick bay, tossing vainly to prevent raw buttocks from coming into contact with anything.

I was, for my first two years at the school, the only Hausa-speaking boy in my form, although there were several others in other forms. At first, there is no denying, my Sagresan classmates regarded me as their inferior, and my Sagresan room-mates as an uncultured intruder who needed civilizing. I cannot tell where I found the good sense to take all this in good part; but I learned somehow to rely on my conviction that sooner or later I should prove my worth by my own efforts, and wring from all concerned full acceptance as an equal. I learned, painfully, to smile the smile of unruffled composure when the language in classroom or dormitory changed, in my presence, from English to Sagresan and I sensed that I was its subject. This pretence became unnecessary after the end of the first year, for by then I could understand and speak Sagresan perfectly, and give as good as I got.

But I believe that it was not only my capacity for taking a joke against myself and my people which led to my rapid acceptance in that schoolboy society – and perhaps not even mainly this. The two achievements which I soon found commanded most respect in the school were success in classwork, and having the funds to dress like a sporting young toff. The first requirement I did not find it difficult to meet, as I was soon at the top of the form. As for the second, it was fortunate for my reputation at school that my parents' livelihood was constantly improving, and I was always able to hold my own when it came to dressing in the style considered elegant amongst us then. Trouser turn-ups were beneath notice if they measured less than a foot in width or less than two inches in depth. An Edwardian touch came in with the straw boaters, which were part of the formal school uniform, and, when rained upon, sagged limply like wet socks around our ears.

Very little importance was attached to games and sports at that time, fortunately for me; for I was exceedingly maladroit at most activities of that nature. We were occasionally required to go out cross-country running, proceeding down a rocky slope near the school, through the shallow waters of a creek, up the other side, and around a peninsula. We all had to turn out for this, including the lame, halt and blind, so the pace was not hot; and the only harm done was the whetting of appetites which school food, like school food everywhere, usually failed to satisfy.

In view of my later experience of inter-tribal dissensions in Africa, this early proof of the unifying effect of common objects, a common education, and sharing living, on divergent origins and tribal backgrounds, was to be of the utmost importance to me. After that first term there was nothing in my speech or the cut of my clothes (as there had never been anything in the colour of my skin or in my physical features) to distinguish me from any other boy in the lower school; and, my name apart, no one, however observant, could in the second term have picked me out as not being a Sagresan.

Thus the Sagresan boys – and their parents – accepted me fully into their society soon enough. The girls were, however, a somewhat tougher proposition. I remember walking down Prince Henry Street one evening during my second year at the school, in company with one of the seniors from the North. I had at that time not yet developed much more than a whistling interest in girls, being then still conscious of my need to put in extra work, especially at English, in order to make up for the late start I had had as compared with my classmates. My friend Kodjo, however, was older and not quite so ingenuous as I was; moreover, he said he thought he knew one of the two girls who, in their starched school uniforms, were strolling ahead of us. We quickened our pace until we were walking, silently, a step or two behind them. Kodjo swore later that they had seen the pursuit out of the corners of their eyes and had obligingly slowed down. I cannot vouch for this. I do know that at that moment Kodjo allowed the excitement of the moment to get the better of him, and spoke to me in Hausa. The effect was immediate. Without even looking round at us, the ladies indulged in a contemptuous and prolonged sucking of the

H

teeth, and quickened their steps to a pace which even Kodjo felt it imprudent to match.

This incident hurt nothing in me but my pride. For it was not until the school holidays immediately following it that I was sent for by my parents in Dapo. Membership of any secret society was strictly forbidden by the mission which was educating me; and the missionaries believed at the time that I was merely going home for my first visit to my parents since coming to Sagresa. It was ironical, I have often thought since, that it was necessary for me to come to Sagresa in order to be able to enter Dapo. Such a subterfuge would have been impossible had I remained under the close surveillance of Miss Schwartz and Miss Costello in the missionary bungalow in Lokko.

So I entered a hothouse in which, for six weeks, the pace of my physical and mental development from boyhood into manhood was deliberately quickened. This was done so effectively that I entered the society's groves a child and emerged an adult. My sisters all underwent a similar preparation for adulthood in Dapo, the female secret society. The English girl becomes a woman the day she puts on her first brassière, the Songhaian the day she graduates from this society.

As for the boys, we were trained to become skilful soldiers, husbands and fathers. Many other highly disciplined apprenticeships were served, so that we might play our parts worthily as custodians of the tribe's physical and cultural heritage. We were taught to drum, to sing, and to dance. We learned the tribe's history and its store of folk tales and proverbs. We were shown the way to its sacred shrines and relics. Above all, we were made to swear eternal loyalty to all our brothers and sisters in the tribe, and to our ancestors and gods.

Back to school from Lokko and Dapo, and to four more years of single-minded study. I found now that time was racing by fleet-footed, and the School Certificate Examina-

tion, which to every secondary-school child in British
Africa appeared then the supreme challenge to human
endeavour, drew quickly nearer. During my last year in
school I worked at my books at least ten hours a day. The
picture I kept in my mind's eye was the one my father's
first letter to me had evoked. I was making progress up
my palm tree. The anxious eyes were watching me from
below, the patient prize awaited me above – to be shared,
not gorged. If I looked elsewhere than at what I was
doing the disaster which would result would be wide-
spread. So I gave myself completely to the task in hand.
When my parents sent me pocket-money, I would save
as much as I could to pay for extra coaching in the subjects in which I was weakest. I mixed with as many pupils
from other secondary schools as I could, not for the sake
of their company, but in order to discover from them
who were the best teachers in their schools. Then, un-
beknown to my own teachers, I would make private
arrangements for such coaching as I felt I needed. This all
meant extra homework and added strain, but I learned
to gauge nicely each day just how far my brain could be
driven, and to stop work in good time. My sole recreation
during this period was walking in the hills and swimming
at the beaches; and I trained myself to relax completely
and banish from my mind all thoughts connected with
studies whilst I was away from my books. I had many
friends now, and could always find company for my out-
ings when I wanted it.

The truth was that, far from my being alone in my
obsession with preparing for this examination, almost
every other candidate for it was devoting a similar amount
of time and energy to such a preparation. It is impossible
for anyone who has not been a pupil in a secondary school
in Africa to visualize just what the School Certificate
Examination means to us. If you pass it, not only will
you be able to secure relatively well-paid employment

almost immediately in business or the civil service, but you will be admitted to the select ranks of the 'educated minority', the 'intelligentsia' who are the pride and joy of their relatives and friends and the despair of the Colonel Blimps of British imperialism. We were all fully conscious of this, and the determination to satisfy the exacting requirements of the examining bodies of the University of Cambridge became an all-consuming passion. In spite of all the advice we received to the contrary from teachers and parents, most of us burned a large volume of midnight oil at our studies. Our hurricane lamps became amongst our most prized possessions, secreted away during the day in all kinds of odd corners against discovery by housemasters, parents or guardians. I have often wondered since how we escaped doing permanent injury to our eyesight by this practice, particularly as so much of our 'studying' consisted in reading over and over again sentences and formulae until we had committed them to memory.

It was during my final year at secondary school that I first developed the interest in politics which was later on to be the supreme influence in shaping the course of my life. I was secretary of the school Debating Society, and with our usual love of long and erudite-sounding words, we had framed a motion for debate one week which promised good sport – 'That municipal government in this town is democratic in form and gerontocratic in fact.' We had often laughed amongst ourselves at the ripe old average age of councillors, aldermen and all others in positions of authority or influence in Sagresa; and one of our stock jokes was that amongst the requirements for any sort of promotion to high municipal office was to hold the School Certificate and to be long in the tooth. The motion was proposed by the only municipal councillor we had been able to find who was under forty, and was seconded by the senior prefect of the school. To oppose it we invited a seventy-three-year-old alderman, who had as his seconder the oldest pupil in the school (a fifth-former who was the proud possessor of a birth certificate which was carefully kept out of sight of the principal and the staff, since it revealed his age as twenty-seven; and whose son was rumoured to bring him a packed lunch to school every day).

The president of the Debating Society and I had had considerable difficulty in persuading the councillor and alderman to take part in the debate at all; and the whole school had been warned beforehand both by the principal and by the senior prefects that due regard must be paid to the status of the two guest speakers, and that there was to be no attacking of municipal greybeards generally. The warning was heeded, and our guests were heard with deference. Perhaps the warning was unnecessary, for Africans generally have a deep and ingrained respect for old age, and even when we can find nothing to admire in an old man, we will not easily forget that his grey hairs have earned him the right to courtesy and politeness. So all the heckling was reserved for our own twenty-seven-year-old. Shouts of 'Methuselah' and 'Grandpa', and attempts to put a walking-stick in his hand and a pair of spectacles on his nose, punctuated his speech, and entirely destroyed the effects of any eloquence he might have been producing. He was, however, a good sport, and took it all in excellent spirit. (Later on he was to become the object of admiring envy to many hundreds of school children in Sagresa by walking off with a Grade 1 School Certificate.)

But for me the significance of that debate lay not in the eminence of our guest speakers or the thick skin of 'Grandpa', but in the sad truth which, as we all knew well enough, the motion contained. As I sat taking notes of the speeches, I wondered again and again whether it was really necessary to live so long before one was qualified to make a useful contribution to public affairs in one's town or village. One of the speakers in support of the motion had collected an impressive array of facts and figures from other African countries to prove his point; and he certainly succeeded in making it appear that more importance was attached to age in our town than was the case elsewhere on the continent. The member of staff who was chairman for the occasion carefully kept the debate from going off course, and speakers were prevented from discussing whether any progress towards the magic goal of self-government was possible under the rule of old men; but certainly it was in precisely this direction that I found my thoughts turning again and again. Until that afternoon I had found myself too absorbed in my studies to give more than a passing thought to politics, municipal or national. But in that somewhat flippant debate I thought I caught a fleeting glimpse of two great truths which have remained with me since. The first was that a constitution on paper can be a very different thing from a constitution in practice, because social attitudes are far more important than ordinances and laws in determining the effective shape of a government. The second truth I glimpsed was that the older a man gets the less disposed he is to change the political system to which he is accustomed and that therefore if national development requires radical political change, as is the case in subject territories, sooner or later the centre of political influence must be made to shift from the older generation to the younger.

Having thought thus far, I cannot remember pursuing the matter any farther at the time, either in word, deed or thought. I had glimpsed what might have been a mere mirage, and was soon plodding again devotedly across the arid wastes of the School Certificate syllabus, towards a more immediate and more tangible goal. But even mirages leave their mark on the mind; and some of the speeches made at that debate were to return to me with crystal clarity during my student days, when we were analysing with the usual student intentness the causes of our real or imagined political ills.

Two weeks before the fateful examination began, I was indiscreet enough to fight the principal's son. He was a fellow fifth-former with whom, up till then, I had had no quarrel at all. He was inclined to be a little over-bearing at times; but then a flint needs contact with another flint in order to spark, and I had been forced to develop from the start an easy-going and tolerant dis-position. I suppose as the examination drew nearer our nerves became tauter and our tempers shorter. When during a discussion in our classroom about careers Samuel declared unnecessarily loudly that he believed all persons who came from the North should return to it to find employment, I suddenly felt my anger rising like a column of mercury. I asked him why, in as calm a voice as I could assume; he replied with a sneer by quoting a Sagresan proverb whose meaning was roughly that even a man who does not know where he is going to ought at least to know where he has come from; and the general laughter which greeted it brought my temper to boiling-point. I was tall and well built, but so was he: three strides took me to his side, and one blow floored him. By the time the senior prefect succeeded in separating us, Sagresan blood and Lokko blood had mingled on the floor. Moreover, as is the custom with us, the fight was as much verbal as physical, and a torrent of abuse directed mainly against the other's antecedents was flowing out of each battered mouth.

We were bloody, sweaty, and dusty when it was over, but still only partly through our respective stocks of abuse. Nothing more than a heightened respect each for the other might have come out of the fight had Samuel been a boarder. Unfortunately, for both of us, however, he lived very much under his august father's eye, and the marks I had succeeded in leaving on his face were too

distinctive to be hidden by any sort of artifice. I prepared
for the worst (prepared in spirit, that is, for physical
preparations were known to be unavailing at such times).
The summons to the Principal's office duly came after
lunch that same day.

He was quite impartial, I'll say that for him. We were
both arched over his desk and inscribed across our rumps
with two dozen strokes of a bamboo four-footer. Then we
were made to shake hands with each other and sent off
for a walk together along the beach and back (this was
the Principal's usual way of dealing with a pair of fighters,
and one which usually made bosom friends of them). That
thrashing, and the walk which followed, gave me the
moments of deepest mortification I have experienced, and
drove home to me the utter futility and wastefulness of
making issues of tribal divisions, in a land where so much
else required our attentions and our energies. Having
heard from us how the fight started, the Principal might
so easily have wasted our time and his, reading us a long
patriotic sermon on the essential brotherhood of all the
people of Songhai. Such a theme would have made him
appear to me a hypocrite and to Samuel a traitor – for we
both knew only too well that the differences between us
were real, if not deep. Instead, we were made to share a
fellowship of misery and humiliation which linked us together more effectively than any half-believed fiction about
cultural or ethnic affinities could have succeeded in doing.

So we walked in silence along that beach under a
burnished sky, lost in thoughts which we were later to
discover were very similar. We were only half-conscious
of the presence behind us of one of the school prefects
who had been detailed by the Principal to dog our footsteps (and report any failure to complete our penance).
After this we avoided each other for a whole week, not
out of spite but out of embarrassment. It was only after
this feeling had worn off, and the curious questionings and

malicious sallies which the incident had inspired in our classmates has begun to wear thin, that Samuel and I saw in each other's eyes across the chapel aisle one evening a message in response to which we met afterwards in an empty classroom. What passed between us then was more, much more, than mere reconciliation; more even than the making and sealing of what was to become a life-long friendship – though certainly both these were achieved. Far more important was the joint pledging of ourselves to an ideal of helping to create in our time a country which would achieve both strength and freedom through unity, and the subordination to that ideal of all tribal loyalties. That we both remained entirely faithful to that ideal will, I believe, be seen from the rest of my story.

So the examination came and passed; and the results which were published after a seemingly interminable period of waiting showed that the long hours of study had not been in vain. 'Grandpa', Samuel and I were amongst the proud holders of first-grade certificates, and this meant that the way was open for us to win scholarships for university studies. I had hardly thought about this possibility, mainly because I was doubtful as to whether my English had yet reached a sufficiently high standard. The evening the results came out, Samuel and I walked up to the top of College Hill to reflect on next steps. A silver filigree of stars was above our heads, a golden filigree of lights at our feet. The moon was rising and full, and had thrown a glittering silver coin into the fountain by which we sat. We sang, sang at the top of our powerful young lungs, in sheer relief and exhilaration. Cars, buses and pedestrians passed us on their way to and from the university college which was housed in brand-new buildings on the slopes of the hill. A passing group of students offered to fetch us the college doctor. But we could afford to laugh back with them and to continue our song.

Near the upper limit of the college site, there was a

small amphitheatre. Samuel and I took the stage and acted to an invisible audience as much of *Macbeth* (one of our set-books) as we could remember. This was not, I think, to get it out of our systems, for we both had developed a genuine affection for Shakespeare. We wished finally to prove to ourselves that the examiner's assessment of our intelligence and knowledge had been entirely accurate. We were at the zenith of self-conceit.

When we re-emerged, somewhat hoarse and dusty, it was late. A near-by college staff bungalow glowed with cosy light, and the sounds of B.B.C. community hymn-singing reached us from its open windows, to be strangely echoed by the rediffusion loudspeakers in humbler households in the town below. The moon was now high in the sky, silvering the very air we breathed. To our right, and forming a bizarre accompaniment to the hymns, the sound of drumming rose throbbing from a near-by village. Both of us realized the symbolism of our position in place and time; buffeted by confused cross-currents of native and alien cultures, standing excitedly on the fringes of academic life. We stood there for a moment, silent and thoughtful. Then we turned and made our way back to town in a mood no less elated, though much less boisterously so.

ONUORA NZEKWU

ONUORA NZEKWU was born in Kafanchan, Northern Nigeria, in 1928. After having attended various schools in Northern and Eastern Nigeria, he became a teacher and afterwards editor of *Nigerian Magazine*. He has written two novels, *Wand of Noble Wood* and *Blade among the Boys*.

The theme of *Blade Among the Boys* is carnal sexuality found in ancestral rites as opposed to Roman Catholicism and its anti-carnal concept for the noviciate priest. Patrick Ikenga is a modern Nigerian caught between two fires in his position as Okpala, the spiritual head of his dead and living family, and a young noviciate. This clash leads ultimately to his downfall. The excerpt below shows the futile efforts of his mother to prevent his becoming a priest because of what she considers to be a shameful celibacy.

The Mother

Veronica Ikenga was shown into the reception hall and Patrick was sent for. As soon as she set eyes on him she cried:

'Why did you do this to me?'

'Mother, can't I ever make a decision for myself without you or Uncle Ononye butting in trying to make me what you think best?'

She looked surprised.

'So that's how it is! So you must decide to ruin the life which your father and I gave you! Have you thought what a terrible thing you are doing, trying to put an end to the family? Did it ever occur to you that by your action you would be making all your relations objects of ridicule in the whole of Ado? Hasn't it ever occurred to you that your action will give rise to all sorts of gossip, including such rumours as that you are a eunuch or a slave? What precedence is there to warrant this action which you have taken?'

'I guess there is none, but what is wrong with my setting the pace for others to follow?'

'Have you considered,' she asked, lowering her voice, 'that you are setting the whole of your paternal relations against me because they believe that you did this with my consent? Have you realized that you are killing me?'

'You know that I would never dream of doing such a thing, Mother,' he answered.

'Then leave this place and come home with me.'

'No, Mother.'

'My son, you know I love you and will willingly give my life to make you happy. I only ask one thing of you. Come with me and marry and produce only two children who'll keep the family going and I shall be satisfied. In so doing, you will exonerate me at your lineage tribunal; you'll prove to the world that you are no eunuch and we shall all be happy. We shall each go our various ways; you to the priesthood and I to look after my daughter-in-law and my grandchildren.'

'No one becomes a priest after marriage. You know, Mother, I don't see why you should worry very much, seeing that God Himself has called me to serve Him. I have made all arrangements for your welfare and your comfort and I am sure you'll want for nothing. I have put by for you three thousand pounds and every month the bank will give you enough to make you live like a queen.'

'Your money is no use to me without you. You asked why I worry so much. I'll tell you. It is because I am trying to save you from committing the worst crime anyone can commit in Ado – that of letting one's family fold up as if there is no one to keep it going. Time was, not long ago, when in families where there were no boys a girl volunteered, or was prevailed upon, not to marry. She lived in her father's house and reproduced for the family. Wives who were unfortunate not to give birth to sons encouraged their husbands to marry second, third and even fourth wives, so that one of them might be the saviour of the situation. Always the emphasis has been on the having of children, especially boys, who would properly ensure the continuity of the life of the family. And here you are, shirking the responsibility which even God Himself has assigned you, and you call yourself a man!'

She paused, tears streaming down her face.

'Listen,' she continued. 'I want John Ikenga's family to continue. It must continue. I do not want you to be the last of it. I need a son to continue the work of reproduction in the family. I do not see why it must not when I have got you to do it.'

'All right, Mother, I've heard you,' Patrick said. 'It is a big problem you have posed for me. I must have time to think it over.'

Just then the bell rang in the distance. It was the bell calling all the students to the refectory for lunch. Patrick told his mother so.

'You go and eat,' she said. 'That will give you enough time to arrive at a decision. I am waiting here for you, so please come back soon.'

Patrick left her and she became engrossed with her own thoughts. She didn't notice the passing of time. When at last she came out of her reverie the clock on the wall chimed 4.30 p.m. She became suspicious and went traight to the Principal's office.

'Where is my boy?' she asked, as soon as she threw open the door.

'Isn't he supposed to be with you?' the Principal countered.

'Yes, but he went for lunch and promised to come back in half an hour.'

'In that case, I'll send for him. I guess he must be in the chapel.'

She strode out of the office and walked towards the chapel. Patrick was not there. A boy told her he had just left for the reception hall. She hurried to the reception hall but Patrick was not there. She went back to the Principal's office but he was gone. She tried to find out who was next in command but none of the students would talk to her because the silent hour had just begun. She didn't know what to do and it was getting late for her to remain at Uchi, where she knew no one. She thought for a while and decided that no useful purpose would be served by her remaining in the compound; so she left and returned to Ado.

Early the next morning she went back to Uchi and made her way to the seminary. She had tried being con-stitutional but it didn't work. Now she had a new idea. Arrived there, she went to the Principal's office and sat on the doorstep. Then she began shouting at the top of her voice:

'Fathers, give me back my son. . . . You cannot snatch him away from me. . . . I am his mother and I do not want to sacrifice him as your mothers have sacrificed you! . . .'

Her shouts attracted the attention of the passers-by – men going to work, children going to school and women going to market. A little crowd of women gathered by the wayside sympathizing with her. Her voice carried to them loud and clear and they all wondered why her son should be accepted as a seminarian against her will.

'Why must you seduce my only child? . . . Why must you make him a eunuch? . . . If you knew the pains of childbirth you wouldn't have dared to take him from me.'

She shouted all day, resting when she became tired and going on after she had rested. Her shouts disturbed the work in the Principal's office and lectures in the class-rooms. Sometimes she was crying, sometimes laughing. Sometimes she said things that were funny, sometimes things that were serious and weighty. The Principal, members of staff and even students talked to her, but she would not listen. She wanted her son. In the evening she went home.

The next morning she was there again, shouting as loud as she could. When they closed the office doors she moved to one of the classroom buildings and when the classes were over she walked between the dormitories and the Principal's residence, shouting and disturbing their siesta. Children walking along the road thought she was mad and wondered why she was not chained at home, and why, of all places, she chose the seminary for her shouting-sprees.

On this second day the Principal decided to talk to her again but she was not prepared to listen to any talk. All she wanted was her son, but her son was not willing to go with her.

When she returned on the third morning Patrick was ready for her. He had given much thought to the question at night and had decided on a show-down with her. The seminarians had just finished breakfast and were leaving the refectory when she started shouting again. Patrick was in the company of two other seminarians.

'There she goes,' he commented, as soon as he heard her voice. 'She doesn't think she has made enough nuisance of herself yet. Excuse me.'

He left the two other men and made for the Principal's office. This morning his mother began with a narrative

She shouted all day, resting when she became tired and going on after she had rested

of what injustices he had suffered at the hands of the
missionaries as a schoolboy. Then she asked, 'Why
must you now draw him out of a good job with the
Railway and try to render him useless after he recovered
from the paralysing blow struck him at Holy Trinity
College?'

Just as she had finished that question, she saw Patrick
coming towards her.

'Have they released you?' she asked, rising. 'Where are
your things? Get them and let's go.'

'Go home, Mother. This is no place for you. For three
days now you have made yourself a nuisance in this
compound. Do you see other women coming and dis-
gracing themselves like this here?'

'Come with me and I'll no longer be a menace to them.'

'I cannot come with you. Why don't you leave me
alone?'

She stretched out a hand towards him and he moved
back from it. 'Don't touch me,' he warned.

This warning broke down her reserve of energy. Slowly
she sank back on the steps and cried. Her whole frame
shook with the despair that hit her then. Memories of the
loss of her husband and of all she had suffered for her
boy came crowding back in her mind and made her cry
as she had done only once before – when her husband died.
Patrick watched her for a while and was touched by her
weeping. Then it dawned on him that it was not her
fault. He knew what fears drove her to do the things she
was doing. He went forward and sat beside her. He put
an arm round her shaking shoulders and tried to comfort
her. It was some time before she could exercise control
over herself.

When at last she did she sat quietly, staring blankly
into space, her right arm across her lap, her right hand
supporting the elbow of the left arm which reached up
to support in a cupped hand the jaw of her head, slightly

tilted to one side. Her tear-stained face was pathetic to behold. Silent voices were whispering to her.

'Rise,' they advised. 'Get hold of his pants. Never let go. Beat him up. Carry him away and chain him up so that he'll never leave you again. Do anything, but don't let him get away this time.'

She rose slowly and Patrick stood up too. The voices were urging her more and more to get hold of his pants and never let go when Patrick spoke.

'Mother,' he said. 'I am sorry you feel this way about my going into the priesthood. I had thought it would gladden your heart, seeing that you and my father gave your approval to it many years ago. You've got to get used to the fact that I am no longer a small child. If I were married I should be having a family of my own now, and you wouldn't be barging in on us to give us directions as to how to live our lives. Why won't you let me be free like the full-grown man that I am?'

'Take pity on me and come home with me,' she pleaded.

'No, Mother. I have been called by God to become His priest and I cannot resist Him.'

'Please, Patrick. This must be the devil's voice that you heard. If God called you, He would have spoken to me, too.'

The boy was silent.

'Are you coming with me?'

'No, Mother, I can't.'

Then she spoke with surprising vehemence. 'Since you have chosen to become a priest without my permission, since you have decided to waste your life for nothing, since you have decided to resist me, to make your relations the laughing-stock of the people of Ado, know that you no longer have me for your mother. I myself know that I no longer have a son. And, mark my words, if you ever get to become a priest it will be as though through a process of boiling over fire.'

She burst into tears again, turned round and picked her way out of the compound. Patrick stood spellbound on the steps of the office. His mother was almost at the gate when the meaning of what she had said dawned on him. He went down the steps three at a time and raced after her, calling to her. She walked on and was passing through the gate when he called again.

'Mother! Mother!'

She did not turn and, just as he reached the gate, she had crossed it into the street on the other side of the fence. He stood at the gate watching her receding figure, conscious that a vacuum had been created in his life by her walking out on him. He had hoped that she would understand but he had been mistaken, and now the only one left to him in this wide, wide world had also turned her back on him. He watched her until she took the bend on the road before he turned and returned slowly to his lessons.

Mrs Ikenga never recovered from the shock of losing her son. She had hoped that her shouts would make the priests send the boy away from the seminary. But after what had happened at the seminary that day she knew that it was not the priests who were taking her son from her but her son who had elected to abandon her. A few days after her return she became ill. Her condition grew worse every day. Two weeks later she was admitted into a hospital, and four weeks after that she died.

NOTES

John Ikenga : Patrick Ikenga's father

ALSO BY ONUORA NZEKWU

Wand of Noble Wood (Hutchinson, 1961)

JAMES NGUGI

JAMES NGUGI was born in Kenya and has recently graduated with Honours in English from Makerere University College in Kampala, Uganda. His short stories have appeared in *Pen-Point*, *Transition* and *New African*. His play has been produced at the National Theatre in Uganda and his first novel, *Weep not, Child*, was published earlier this year.

This story, *The Martyr*, is set during the Mau Mau Emergency in Kenya. It is a study of the relationship and misunderstanding between the patronizing white settler Mrs Hill, and her servant Njoroge, who is torn between loyalty to the cause and loyalty towards his conscience.

The Martyr

When Mr and Mrs Garstone were murdered in their home by unknown gangsters, there was a lot of talk about it. It was all in the front page of the daily papers and figured importantly in the Radio Newsreel. Perhaps this was so because they were the first European settlers to be killed in the increased wave of violence that had spread all over the country. The violence was said to have political motives. And wherever you went, in the market-places, in the Indian bazaars, in a remote African duka, you were bound to hear something about the murder. There were a variety of accounts and interpretations.

Nowhere was the matter more thoroughly discussed than in a remote, lonely house built on a hill, which belonged, quite appropriately, to Mrs Hill, whose husband, an old veteran settler of the pioneering period, had died the previous year after an attack of malaria, while on a visit to Uganda. Her only son and daughter were now getting their education at 'Home' – home being another name for England. Being one of the earliest settlers and owning a lot of land with big tea plantations sprawling right across the country, she was much respected by the others if not liked by all.

For some did not like what they considered her too 'liberal' attitude to the 'natives'. When Mrs Smiles and Mrs Hardy came into her house two days later to discuss the murder, they wore a look of sad triumph – sad because Europeans (not just Mr and Mrs Garstone) had been killed, and of triumph, because the essential depravity and ingratitude of the natives had been demonstrated beyond all doubt. No longer could Mrs Hill maintain that natives could be civilized if only they were handled in the right manner.

Mrs Smiles was a lean, middle-aged woman whose tough, determined nose and tight lips reminded one so vividly of a missionary. In a sense she was. Convinced that she and her kind formed an oasis of civilization in a wild country of savage people, she considered it almost her calling to keep on reminding the natives and anyone else of the fact, by her gait, talk and general bearing.

Mrs Hardy was of Boer descent and had early migrated into the country from South Africa. Having no opinions of her own about anything, she mostly found herself agreeing with any views that most approximated those of her husband and her race. For instance, on this day, she found herself in agreement with whatever Mrs Smiles said. Mrs Hill stuck to her guns and maintained, as indeed she had always done, that the natives were obedient at heart and *all* you needed was to treat them kindly.

'That's all they need. *Treat them kindly*. They will take kindly to you. Look at my "boys". They all love me. They would do anything I ask them to!' That was her philosophy and it was shared by quite a number of the liberal, progressive type. Mrs Hill had done some liberal things to her 'boys'. Not only had she built some brick quarters (*brick*, mind you) but had also put up a school for the children. It did not matter if the school had not enough teachers or if the children learnt only half a day and worked in the plantations for the other half; it was more than most other settlers had the courage to do!

'It is horrible. Oh, a horrible act,' declared Mrs Smiles rather vehemently. Mrs Hardy agreed. Mrs Hill remained neutral.

'How could they do it? We've brought 'em civilization. We stopped slavery and tribal wars. Were they not all leading savage miserable lives?' Mrs Smiles spoke with all her powers of oratory. Then she concluded with a sad shake of the head. 'But I've always said they'll never be civilized, simply can't take it.'

'We should show tolerance,' suggested Mrs Hill. Her tone spoke more of the missionary than Mrs Smiles's looks.

'Tolerant! Tolerant! How long shall we continue being tolerant? Who could have been more tolerant than the Garstones? Who more kind? And to think of all the squatters they maintained!'

'Well, it isn't the squatters who —'

'Who did? Who did?'

'They should all be hanged!' suggested Mrs Hardy. There was conviction in her voice.

'And to think they were actually called from bed by their houseboy!'

'Indeed?'

'Yes. It was their houseboy who knocked at their door

and urgently asked them to open. Said some people were
after him —'

'Perhaps there —'

'No! It was all planned. All a trick. As soon as the door
was opened, the gang rushed in. It's all in the paper.'

Mrs Hill looked away rather guiltily. She had not read
her paper.

It was time for tea. She excused herself and went near
the door and called out in a kind, shrill voice,

'Njoroge! Njoroge!'

Njoroge was her houseboy. He was a tall, broad-
shouldered person nearing middle age. He had been
in the Hills' service for more than ten years. He wore
green trousers, with a red clothband round the waist and
a red fez on the head. He now appeared at the door and
raised his eyebrows in inquiry – an action which with him
accompanied the words 'Yes, Memsahib?' or 'Ndio,
Bwana.'

'Leta Chai.'

'Ndio, Memsahib!' and he vanished back after casting
a quick glance round all the Memsahibs there assembled.
The conversation which had been interrupted by Njoroge's
appearance was now resumed.

'They look so innocent,' said Mrs Hardy.

'Yes. Quite the innocent flower but the serpent under
it.' Mrs Smiles was acquainted with Shakespeare.

'Been with me for ten years or so. Very faithful. Likes
me very much.' Mrs Hill was defending her boy.

'All the same I don't like him. I don't like his face.'

'The same with me.'

Tea was brought. They drank, still chatting about the
death, the government's policy, and the political demagogues who were undesirable elements in this otherwise
beautiful country. But Mrs Hill, with a great conviction
that almost carried the point through, maintained that
these semi-illiterate demagogues who went to Britain and

thought they had education did not know the true aspirations of their people. You could still win your boys by being kind to them.

Nevertheless, when Mrs Smiles and Mrs Hardy had gone, she brooded over that murder and the conversation. She felt uneasy and for the first time noticed that she lived a bit too far from any help in case of an attack. The knowledge that she had a pistol was a comfort.

Supper was over. That ended Njoroge's day. He stepped out of the light into the countless shadows and then vanished into the darkness. He was following the footpath from Mrs Hill's house to the workers' quarters down the hill. He tried to whistle to dispel the silence and loneliness that hung around him. He could not. Instead he heard the owl cry.

He stopped, stood stock-still. Below, he could perceive nothing. But behind him, the immense silhouette of Memsahib's house – large, imposing – could be seen. He looked back intently, angrily. In his anger, he suddenly thought he was growing old.

'You. You. I've lived with you so long. And you've reduced me to this! In my own land! What have I got from you in return?' Njoroge wanted to shout to the house all this and many other things that had long accumulated in his heart. The house would not respond. He felt foolish and moved on.

Again the owl cried. Twice!

'A warning to her,' Njoroge thought. And again his whole soul rose in anger – anger against all those with a white skin, all those foreign elements that had displaced the true sons of the land from their God-given place. Had God not promised Gekoyo that he would give all the land to the father of the tribe – he and his posterity? Now all the land had been taken away.

He remembered his father as he always did when these moments of anger and bitterness possessed him. He had

died in the struggle – the struggle to rebuild the destroyed
shrines. That was at the famous Nairobi Massacre when
police fired on a people peacefully demonstrating for their
right. His father was among the people who died. Since then
Njoroge had had to struggle for a living – seeking employment here and there on European farms. He had met many
types – some harsh, some kind, but all dominating, giving
him just what salary they thought fit for him. Then he had
come to be employed by the Hills. It was a strange co-
incidence that he had come here. A big portion of the land
now occupied by Mrs Hill was the land his father had
always shown him as belonging to the family. They had
found the land occupied when his father and some of the
others had temporarily retired to Muranga owing to
famine. They had come back and *Ng'o!* the land was gone.

'Do you see that fig tree? Remember that land is yours.
Be patient. Watch these Europeans. They will go and then
you can claim the land.'

He was then small. After his father's death, Njoroge had
forgotten all about this injunction. But when he co-
incidentally came here and saw the tree, he had remembered. He knew it all – all by heart. He knew where every
boundary went through.

Njoroge had never liked Mrs Hill. He had always
resented her complacency in thinking she had done so
much for the workers. He had worked with cruel types
like Mrs Smiles and Mrs Hardy. But he always knew
where he stood with such. But Mrs Hill! Her liberalism
was almost smothering. Njoroge hated all settlers. He
hated above all what he thought was their hypocrisy and
self-satisfaction. He knew that Mrs Hill was no exception.
She was like all the others, only she loved paternalism. It
convinced her she was better than the others. But she was
worse. You did not know exactly where you stood with her.

All of a sudden, Njoroge shouted, 'I hate them! I hate
them!' Then a grim satisfaction came over him. Tonight,

anyway, Mrs Hill would die – pay for her own smug liberalism or paternalism and pay for all the sins of her settlers' race. It would be one settler less.

He came to his own room. All the other rooms belonging to the other workers had stopped smoking. The lights had even gone out in many of them. Perhaps, some were already asleep or gone to the Native Reserve to drink beer. He lit the lantern and sat on the bed. It was a very small room. Sitting on the bed one could almost touch all the corners of the room if one stretched the arms afar. Yet it was here, *here*, that he with two wives and a number of children had to live, had in fact lived for more than five years. So crammed! Yet Mrs Hill thought that she had done enough by just having the houses built with brick.

'*Mzun sana*, eh?' (very good, eh?) she was very fond of asking. And whenever she had visitors she brought them to the edge of the hill and pointed at the houses.

Again Njoroge smiled grimly to think now Mrs Hill would pay for all this self-congratulatory piety. He also knew that he had an axe to grind. He had to avenge the death of his father and strike a blow for the occupied family land. It was a foresight on his part to have taken his wives and children back to the Reserve. They might else have been in the way and in any case he did not want to bring trouble to them should he be forced to run away after the act.

The other Jhii (Freedom Boys) would come at any time now. He would lead them to the house. Treacherous – yes! But how necessary.

The cry of the owl, this time louder than ever, reached his ears. That was a bad omen. It always portended death – death for Mrs Hill. He thought of her. He remembered her. He had lived with Memsahib and Bwana for more than ten years. He knew that she had loved her husband. Of that he was sure. She almost died of grief when she had learnt of his death. In that moment her settlerism had been shorn off. In that naked moment, Njoroge had been able to pity her. Then the children! He had known them. He had seen them grow up like any other children. Almost like his own. They loved their parents and Mrs Hill had always been so tender with them, so loving. He thought of them in England, wherever that was, fatherless and motherless.

And then he realized, all too suddenly, that he could not do it. He could not tell how, but Mrs Hill had suddenly crystallized into a woman, a wife, somebody like Njen or Wambuu, and above all, a mother. He could not kill a woman. He could not kill a mother. He hated himself for this change. He felt agitated. He tried hard to put himself in the other condition, his former self and see her as just a settler. As a settler, it was all easy. For Njoroge hated settlers and all Europeans. If only he could see her like this (as one among many white men or settlers) then he could do it. Without scruples. But he could not bring back the other self. Not now, anyway. You see, he had never thought of her in these terms. Never! never! Until today. And yet he knew she was the same, and would be the same tomorrow – a patronizing, complacent woman. It was then that he knew that he was a divided man and perhaps would ever remain like that. For now it even seemed an impossible thing to snap just like that ten years of relationship, even though to him they had been years of pain and shame. He prayed and wished there had never been injustices. Then there would never have been this rift – the rift between white and black. Then he would never have been put in this painful situation.

What was he to do now? Would he betray the 'Boys'? He sat there, irresolute, unable to decide on a course of action. If only he had not thought of her in human terms! That he hated settlers was quite clear in his mind. But to kill a mother of two seemed too painful a task for him to do in a free frame of mind.

He went out.

Darkness still covered him and he could see nothing clearly. The stars above seemed to be anxiously awaiting Njoroge's decision. Then, as if their cold stare was compelling him, he began to walk, walk back to Mrs Hill's house. He had decided to save her. Then probably he would go to the forest. There, he would for ever fight with a freer conscience. That seemed excellent. It would also serve as a propitiation for his betrayal of the other 'Boys'.

There was no time to lose. It was already late and the 'Boys' might come any time. So he ran with one purpose – to save the woman. At the road he heard footsteps. He stepped into the bush and lay still. He was certain that those were the 'Boys'. He waited breathlessly for the footsteps to die. Again he hated himself for this betrayal. But how could he fail to hearken to this voice – the true Voice that speaks to all men and women of all races and all times. He ran on when the footsteps had died. It was necessary to run for, if the 'Boys' discovered his betrayal, he would surely meet death. But then he did not mind this. He only wanted to finish this other task first.

At last, sweating and panting, he reached Mrs Hill's house and knocked at the door, crying, 'Memsahib! Memsahib!'

Mrs Hill had not yet gone to bed. She had sat up, a multitude of thoughts crossing her mind. Ever since that afternoon's conversation with the other women, she had felt more and more uneasy. When Njoroge went and she was left alone she had gone to her safe and taken out her pistol, with which she was now toying. It was better to be prepared. It was unfortunate that her husband had died. He might have kept her company.

She sighed over and over again as she remembered her pioneering days. She and her husband and others had tamed the wilderness of this country and had developed a whole mass of unoccupied land. People like Njoroge now lived contented without a single worry about tribal wars. They had a lot to thank the European for.

Yet she did not like those politicians who came to corrupt the otherwise obedient and hard-working men, especially when treated kindly. She did not like this murder of the Garstones. No! She did not like it. And when she remembered the fact that she was really alone, she thought it might be better for her to move down to Nairobi or Kinangop and stay with friends a while.

But what would she do with her boys? Leave them there? She wondered. She thought of Njoroge. A queer boy. Had he many wives? Had he a large family? It was surprising even to her to find that she had lived with him so long, yet had never thought of these things. It was a shock to her. It was the first time she had ever thought of him as a man with a family. She had always seen him as a servant. Even now it seemed ridiculous to think of her houseboy as a father with a family. She sighed. This was an omission, something to be righted in future.

And then she heard a knock on the front door and a voice calling out 'Memsahib! Memsahib!'

It was Njoroge's voice. Her houseboy. Sweat appeared all over her face. She could not even hear what the boy was saying for all the circumstances of the Garstones' death came to her. This was her end. The end of the road. So Njoroge had led them here! She trembled and felt weak.

But all of a sudden, strength came back to her. She knew she was alone. She knew they would break in. No! She would die bravely. Holding her pistol more firmly in her hand, she opened the door and quickly fired. Then a nausea came to her. She had killed a man for the first time. She felt weak and fell down crying, 'Come and kill me!' She did not know that she had in fact killed her saviour. Njoroge was dead.

On the following day, it was all in the papers. That a

single woman could fight a gang fifty strong was bravery unknown. And to think she had killed one too!

Mrs Smiles and Mrs Hardy were especially profuse in their congratulations.

'We told you they're all bad.'

'They are all bad,' agreed Mrs Hardy. Mrs Hill kept quiet. The whole circumstances of Njoroge's death still worried her. The more she thought about it, the more of a puzzle it was to her. She gazed still into space. Then she let out a slow enigmatic sigh.

'I don't know,' she said. 'Oh! I think I *didn't* understand Njoroge.'

'Don't know?'

'Yes. That's it. Inscrutable.' Mrs Smiles was triumphant. 'All of them should be whipped.'

'All of them should be whipped,' agreed Mrs Hardy.

Perhaps none would ever know that Njoroge was a martyr. Nor would anyone ever know that Mrs Hill felt remorse.

NOTES

Boer : one of Afrikaner descent. A white Afrikaans-speaking
    South African
'*Ndio Bwana*' : 'Yes sir'; 'Yes master'
'*Leta Chai*' : 'Bring Tea'
duka : shop
Ng'o : a term of surprise

ALSO BY JAMES NGUGI

Weep not, Child (Heinemann, 1964)
The River Between (Heinemann, 1965)
A Grain of Wheat (Heinemann, 1967)